DOG INSIGHT

Pamela Reid, Ph.D., CAAB

Wenatchee, Washington U.S.A.

Dog InSight
Pamela Reid, Ph.D., CAAB

Dogwise Publishing
A Division of Direct Book Service, Inc.
403 South Mission Street, Wenatchee, Washington 98801
1-509-663-9115, 1-800-776-2665
www.dogwisepublishing.com / info@dogwisepublishing.com

Photos: Nick Burchell
Graphic Design: Lindsay Peternell

The essays in this book originally appeared in *Dogs in Canada.* Used with permission.

Library of Congress Cataloging-in-Publication Data
Reid, Pamela, 1960-
  Dog inSight / Pamela Reid.
    p. cm.
  ISBN 978-1-61781-054-1
  1. Dogs--Behavior. 2. Dogs--Training. I. Title.
  SF433.R45 2012
  636.7--dc23
                            2011032094

ISBN: 978-1-61781-054-1

Printed in the U.S.A.

To my Dad,

Dickson Reid,

who instilled in me a fascination
and respect for all animals.

More praise for *Dog InSight*

Dog InSight is a must-read book for dog owners who seek plainspoken guidance on ways to improve their relationships with their dogs. If your dog has ever quivered with fear at a clap of thunder, forgotten his housetraining skills, or simply befuddled you with his wacky antics, Dr. Reid's insights into the causes of behavioral problems, along with her advice on modification techniques, will prove enlightening. Throughout the book, Dr. Reid debunks myths that have pervaded among dog owners. Readers will no longer fear that playing tug-of-war with their puppies will foster aggressiveness. With her thoughtful approach and real-life examples, Dr. Reid has written a book that is destined to become a resource for dog owners everywhere.

Ed Sayres, President & CEO, American Society for the Prevention of Cruelty to Animals (ASPCA)

As a colleague I have had the pleasure of hearing Pam Reid's insights on dog behavior for a number of years. In her new book, *Dog InSight* she brings her thoughts to a larger audience. Dr. Reid uses common examples of dog behavior familiar to everyone who has shared their life and home with a dog to illustrate our current scientific understanding of dogs and their behavior. At the same time she weaves a compelling story about how her insights can help to ensure that both dogs and people will enjoy being together and doing things together.

Stephen L. Zawistowski, Ph. D., CAAB, Science Advisor, The American Society for the Prevention of Cruelty to Animals

TABLE OF CONTENTS

INTRODUCTION

Have you ever considered what a privilege it is to share your life with a dog? Think about it. Here we are: an advanced primate species—devastating to the environment and feared by most other species on Earth—yet befriended by an innocuous, medium-sized terrestrial carnivore. Clearly, we have a symbiotic relationship. Early in the domestication process, both species benefited from the presence of the other. As we evolved together, the dog served us well as a hunting partner, protector, clean-up crew, and companion. That last function is what makes dogs so unique. Dogs proved to be precious to humans because of their companionship. No two species in the history of the world have come to develop such a friendship as dogs and people.

I'm sure we all have a story about how we came to know the love of a good dog. My story isn't anything special. I grew up as an only child in rural Nova Scotia. I wasn't really an only child; my parents had already raised a family of three when I came along. But I was a lonely child. I had no siblings living at home, and I lived several miles from other children my age. My mom was allergic to animals so I had no pets either. That is, until the day we spied Charlie in the dog catcher's van. Charlie was a Border Collie-ish mutt who spent his days hanging out at the elementary school. No one really knew if he had a home, although in retrospect he wasn't thin or in poor condition, so he probably did. We all adored Charlie, but someone must have called the dog catcher that day, because he staked out the school to nab the trusting dog. Who knew that it would lead to a crowd of kids and our teacher, Mrs. Robinson, swarming around the van, all bawling and pleading for the catcher to release the dog? Drawn into the melee, my mother somehow found herself paying the fine to the dog catcher. Charlie had a new home—and I had a friend. Charlie and I were inseparable until the day I left for university. We roamed the fields and the forests together, we went fishing with my dad, and we covered miles with me on my bike and Charlie by my side. Once Charlie came into the picture, I had an idyllic childhood. My mom adored Charlie too, despite the sneezing that ensured through the next ten years, and she grieved deeply when Charlie died. Charlie graced me with his presence and instilled in me a fascination for all animals. I've been so fortunate to have subsequently shared my life with several incredible dogs.

The dog is a wondrous animal, deserving of our admiration and respect. He is physically powerful—an athlete capable of loping across miles of countryside. He is intensely aware of his surroundings, with hearing much keener than ours, a visual system sensitive to the slightest movements, and a sense of smell we can't even begin to comprehend. His is a rich sensory world that we cannot enter. He is social, preferring companionship to solitude. Left to indulge his whims, the dog will hang out with friends and share information through a complex and subtle system of language to which we are only vaguely privy. He is highly intelligent, though in very specialized ways. The dog is particularly adept at associating his actions with consequences. He is a master of spatial navigation. He is more than capable of learning how to read and cope with his mystifying human partners. To top it all off, the dog is a passionate spirit—always ready for fun, utterly gleeful about life, yet highly sensitive to the emotional states of others. The dog seems to know exactly when a lick or nuzzle will do the trick. He is an ironic little being; I am awed by his power and self-sufficiency on the one hand, yet feel an intense need to protect and nurture him on the other. Although, if I could change one thing, it would be the dog's life span. Dogs' lives are tragically short.

I wrote the information contained in these pages in the hope that readers will share my appreciation and admiration of dogs. These essays are snippets of information and insight into the behaviour of dogs. They originally appeared as columns in the monthly magazine *Dogs in Canada*, and I've loosely partitioned them into three sections—Part 1: Behaviour; Part 2: Training, and Part 3: Behaviour Problems.

Part One

BEHAVIOUR

I am the type of person who can spend an hour just watching the comings and goings of a colony of ants or be utterly captivated by a litter of kittens playing with their mom. So I find it especially hard to fathom that until recently, most behavioural scientists scoffed at the idea of studying the dog as a species. They were considered an "artificial" animal not worthy of our attention. What an absolute shame that we know so little about this complex and fascinating creature that has shared our lives through a significant phase of our evolution. Until fairly recently, all we knew about dogs, from a scientific standpoint, consisted of a handful of anecdotes from famous ethologists such as Charles Darwin and Niko Tinbergen and the groundbreaking work on dog development from John Paul Scott and John Fuller at the Bar Harbor laboratory. Gladly, the tide has shifted and now we are seeing publications on the fundamentals of dog behaviour and cognition. When left to live a feral existence, how do dogs organize themselves into social groups? How do dogs select mating partners and rear their young? Why do dogs urine mark in some spots and not others? What information do dogs glean from other dogs' vocalizations? How do dogs interpret our attempts to communicate with them? Gradually, we are accumulating a respectable body of knowledge about the ethology of the dog. In this section, I touch on some of the basics that would be of general interest, such as canine development, social structure, play and cognition. For more in-depth coverage of dog science, check out these books:

- James Serpell's *The Domestic Dog*
- Per Jensen's *The Behavioural Biology of Dogs*
- Raymond and Laura Coppinger's *Dogs, A New Understanding*
- Ádám Miklósi's *Dog Behaviour, Evolution and Cognition*
- Alexandra Horowitz's *Inside of a Dog*
- John Bradshaw's *Dog Sense*
- Elaine Ostrander, Urs Giger and Kerstin Lindblad-Toh's *The Dog and its Genome*

Brain Waves

The Stages of Your Puppy's Mental Development

There are few things in this world quite as spectacular as the transformation that animals go through in their journey from newborn to adult. The 1965 pioneering work of developmental psychobiologists John Paul Scott and John Fuller—*Genetics and the Social Behavior of Dogs*—provides the foundation for our understanding of the physical and behavioural development of normal puppies. Scott and Fuller divided the progression from birth to sexual maturity in dogs into four distinct periods: neonatal; transition; socialization; and juvenile.

The neonatal period

When canine babies are born, they are completely dependent on their mother for survival. The puppy has a relatively undeveloped brain: the brain waves of a puppy when awake are virtually indistinguishable from those when sleeping. The puppy cannot regulate its own body temperature and is unable to urinate or defecate unless the dam stimulates it. The newborn puppy can feel and taste, but it cannot see or hear. The sense of smell also appears to be non-functional at this age. It can crawl and it can right itself if it topples over. If hungry or cold, the puppy will whine or yelp.

Despite their primitive state, three to ten day old puppies are capable of learning simple associations: a puppy that is given milk after sucking on a rubber nipple will learn to suck more often than if just given water. If the puppy is given a bitter-tasting substance instead of the milk, it will refuse to suck on the nipple.

Experience at this early age can speed up the course of development. Daily handling and other physical contact, including painful events, can lead to increased weight gain, earlier opening of the eyes, and accelerated motor and cognitive development.

The transition period

Significant changes occur over this one week period, although the exact timing varies across breeds and individuals. Eyes open around Day 13, even though the retinas are still undeveloped, and the ability to see emerges gradually over the next few weeks. Puppies start to hear and, by Day 20, show a clear startle response to loud sounds. Teeth begin to come in and puppies try out licking and chewing food. They are increasingly able to maintain their own body temperature. They develop the ability to eliminate on their own and, by the end of this period, are leaving the nest to do their business. They crawl more, then stand and sit upright, and finally take their first steps.

Simple social and play behaviour begin to appear—puppies wag their tails, approach objects, and two week old puppies have been observed to growl over a bone. By three weeks of age, the pups are pawing and mouthing each other.

The ability to learn an association between an event—such as a buzzer, light, or odour—and a mild shock to the puppy's leg, appears around fourteen days. However, a consistent learned reaction does not emerge until the pups are three weeks old. Interestingly, the stimuli that preceded unpleasant shock did not cause an increase in heart rate, leading Scott and Fuller to suggest that at this age, puppies may be protected from the psychological after-effects of a traumatic experience.

The socialization period

The next nine weeks of the puppy's life lead to further refinement of sensory and motor abilities but are primarily a time for social development. Each day brings new discoveries because now all the sensory organs are functional. Puppies begin to run and show more coordinated movements, and they make a greater variety of sounds.

Natural weaning begins around five weeks and is usually complete by ten weeks. House training is best conducted at this age because, by eight to nine weeks, puppies are reluctant to soil their sleeping place.

EEG recordings of brain waves become adult-like by seven to eight weeks and puppies at this stage are sponges for learning. They are now capable of detecting more complex associations. At this age, puppies readily learn that a sound, such as "pup, pup" or a click, predicts food or attention. Learning is limited primarily by their clumsy motor skills.

Puppies become strongly attached to the nesting place at this age and are intensely disturbed if removed. This process, called localization, peaks at around six to seven weeks, after which the puppies are more comfortable with new surroundings.

Aspects of pack behaviour start to appear, including social play and following. The litter may go through a temporary period of ganging up on one puppy. Usually this leads to the formation of an unstable dominance hierarchy amongst the pups around week seven. While sex organs are still undeveloped, puppies will often try out mounting and clasping during play.

Social experiences during this period have a profound and lasting impact on later behaviour. Between three to twelve weeks of age, puppies form strong attachments to both dogs and people. At first, they will approach any person or animal with a wagging tail.

Between five to nine weeks, some puppies become increasingly fearful of unfamiliar people or situations. This wariness, called neophobia, may be overpowered by a social puppy's strong motivation to make contact with people. However, a lack of continued exposure to new experiences can lead to persistent shyness.

These observations led Scott and Fuller to conclude that seven to eight weeks of age is the optimal time to place a puppy in its permanent home. The puppy has received sufficient experience with the dam and littermates to have learned to 'be a dog,' yet it is highly motivated to form lasting relationships with people. A puppy removed from the litter too early may be unable to relate well to other dogs; a puppy removed from the litter too late may be unable to bond well with people.

Some puppies also go through a 'fear period' around nine weeks, making them hypersensitive to distressing events. Physical or psychological trauma at this time can have greater repercussions than if the trauma occurred before or after this fear period.

The juvenile period

This is mainly a period of refining the capabilities and skills that have already emerged. The permanent teeth come in, motor skills become more mature, and growth is less rapid. Learning is limited primarily by the dog's short attention span and heightened excitability. Continued exposure to new people and experiences is necessary through six to eight months of age, as even dogs that were well socialized at three months can regress and become fearful in the absence of continued socialization. There are anecdotal reports of a second phase of hypersensitivity to fearful events around four to six months of age.

Litters left together through this period establish a relatively stable dominance hierarchy. The pet dog often goes through a phase of 'testing' with family members, both human and dog, at this age. Immature sexual behaviour emerges in play.

The juvenile period ends when adult sexual behaviour appears. The female estrous cycle begins and males show leg-lifting, urine-marking, ground-scratching, aggression, roaming, and mounting. Other adult behaviours, such as territorial and protective aggression, coincide with sexual maturity.

Developmental change obviously does not end with the achievement of sexual maturity. Life goes on and with it, comes change. Watching a helpless little baby transform into its final spirit, whether that be a feisty Chihuahua or a powerful Mastiff, is a fascinating experience.

Small Puppies, Big Brains

Giving Your Youngster a Head Start

A few years ago I was asked to evaluate a litter of Australian Shepherd puppies for a potential buyer. As I was ushered into the kitchen to view the pups, I was amazed to see the array of toys and obstacles in their pen. The puppies were chewing on Nylabones, playing with stuffed toys, crawling through tunnels, and climbing on miniature tires and small wooden ramps. Later, as I administered the Puppy Aptitude Test, each puppy demonstrated its willingness to interact with people, explore a novel environment and approach new experiences with confidence and enthusiasm. If I'd been in the market for a puppy, I would have taken one of these budding stars myself. Was there a relationship between the complex puppy pen and the behaviour of these puppies?

Early brain development

Scientific research tells us that good nutrition, good health, and nurturing in early life create the foundation for complex brain development and the ability to think. Certain areas of the brain require stimulation during 'sensitive periods' in order to develop properly. While considerable brain development takes place prior to birth, deprivation and enrichment studies reveal that early experience influences the neural pathways and the 'wiring' of the brain. Humans are born with almost all the neurons they will ever have, but the mass of the infant brain is only about one quarter that of the adult brain. While the brain continues to grow in complexity throughout life, most of its growth occurs in the first three years. At the same time, cells and connections that are not being stimulated waste away. It's not a huge leap to assume the same rapid growth is happening to puppy brains.

Deprivation experiments

Orphans in Romania provide clear evidence to scientists that the brain must be stimulated in early life. Babies who spent most of the first year of their lives lying in cribs suffered abnormally slow development and were unable to achieve their full potential. Some weaknesses were made up with special effort but other deficits were permanent.

Researchers in the 1950s examined the development of a group of Scottish Terriers raised in relative isolation for the first ten months of life. When compared to age-mates raised normally, the isolates were hyperactive, extremely excitable, excessively submissive to other puppies, and very slow to learn. For instance, the puppies were exposed to a novel object that was painful to touch. The normal puppies quickly learned to run away from the object, but the isolate puppies behaved as though they didn't know what to do. When food was concealed under a box, the normal puppies easily figured out how to get at the food, but the isolate puppies couldn't even remember where the food was hidden.

Handling and the stress response

Handling of young animals has been shown to produce a variety of beneficial effects, including accelerated physical development, increased resistance to disease, reduced emotionality and the confidence to explore novel environments. Puppies handled every day are more active, more sociable to humans and more dominant with other dogs in play than puppies handled less often.

Some researchers believe there is a critical period for gaining neural control over the stress response. Baby rats handled for fifteen minutes a day for the first twenty-one days of life were better able to regulate their response to stressful events than non-handled rats. They were better able to learn and even suffered less cognitive impairment as they grew old. Young animals raised without regular handling show sustained levels of stress hormones long after situations that cause the anxiety are over.

Excessive handling is not a good idea, either. Too much handling or chaotic, unpredictable stimulation can adversely affect development. Children exposed to chronic, ongoing stress have trouble controlling their arousal during learning and are unable to cope with novelty. Some animals become sensitized by excessive handling to the point that any tactile contact is perceived as unpleasant.

The impact of early enrichment

If early deprivation has such devastating effects on development, does early enrichment have equally dramatic benefits? On this issue, the evidence is less compelling. The brains of rats and monkeys reared in enriched environments, which included motor, auditory and visual stimulation, show the impact of increased brain activity. After only 80 days in an enriched environment, the connections between neurons were denser and more complex in these animals' brains than the brains of animals reared in normal laboratory cage environments. However, other studies report no change in cortical development.

Author and behaviourist Michael Fox placed previously isolated puppies in enriched environments to see if the effects of early deprivation could be reversed. He observed that the isolate puppies were completely overwhelmed by the new situation, as though they couldn't handle all the sensory input. However, with sustained effort, the puppies improved to the level of normal puppies in many cognitive and social skills.

Enrichment studies with animals sparked the development of initiatives to enhance early social and intellectual development in children. Probably the best known of these is Project Head Start, an intervention program designed to improve opportunities for children from disadvantaged families. After the American government spent millions of dollars and invested enormous effort, the long-term success of Head Start was mixed. There were substantial gains for young African-American children, but these effects were lost as the children became older. In contrast, organized preschool programs in

Sweden and the U.K. produced long-term benefits. Children attending the programs had better vocabularies, were better at reading and mathematics, and had better communication skills, even up to age 13, than children who did not attend the programs. At-risk children benefited from these programs the most.

Head start puppies

Scientific studies do not universally support the statement that extra stimulation during development is beneficial. It may be that the stimulation required for maximal development is what any youngster would receive in an average household. However, none of the research suggests that providing enrichment during development can harm a young animal. At worst, benefits may wash out as the animal matures.

If breeders want their puppies to be all they can be, they should ensure that their pups have the opportunity for good brain development in the early critical weeks of life. Rear the pups in enriched environments, with plenty to stimulate their motor, sensory and cognitive abilities. Handling is a must, ideally with many different people as the puppy develops. Exposure to moderately stressful events, such as removing the pup from the whelping box and placing it on a cold, slippery weigh scale for a short period of time each day, can actually improve the pup's ability to deal with later stressors. Most important, because development continues long after the puppies are with their new families, educate owners on the importance of ongoing socialization, to ensure that the puppies develop into quality companions.

The breeder of those Australian Shepherd puppies was certainly improving the odds that his puppies would develop big, healthy brains. As mature dogs, his pups may have fared no better as intellectual giants than a litter of pups raised in a barn stall, but they were certainly Einsteins as babies. He was determined to give his puppies' brains the best possible head start in life!

THE REAL HIDDEN LIFE OF DOGS

The Dog's Natural Instincts and How to Handle Them

Last winter my dogs found a fresh deer carcass just a few yards off the path we take each morning when exercising. My two dogs, who have eaten nothing but highly processed dog food their entire lives and have managed to dispatch nothing more mighty than the occasional mouse, acted as though this was an all-you-can-eat breakfast buffet set out just for them!

As I watched them helping themselves to this feast, I was struck by how different they behaved than when eating from their bowls in the kitchen. They were acting just like the wild jackals you see on Discovery Channel—they'd rip off a piece and then, while chewing, look around nervously, as though expecting a hyena to appear at any moment to chase them off. For just a few moments, I saw my domesticated dogs as they once were: successful scavengers feeding from the spoils of other hunters. How did they make the transition from natural recycler to pampered house pet?

Domestication

Ray Coppinger, a scientist who studies the evolution of dogs, argues in his book, *Dogs: A Startling New Understanding of Canine Origin, Behaviour, and Evolution,* that dogs are probably like cats in that they 'domesticated' themselves. As people settled into hunter-gatherer communities, the dogs' evolutionary precursor coexisted with them as scavengers, cleaning up the refuse they provided. The dogs were tolerated because they served a valuable cleaning function. The less fearful dogs could be near people and access more food. People were more likely to put up with dogs hanging around if they were not aggressive. So, through a combination of natural and artificial selection, dogs became domesticated to the point that they began to depend on humans for their survival. This was a win-win situation for both dogs and people.

The more traditional view is that ancestral peoples set about to tame the dog's ancestor, presumably by keeping the more tractable animals as guardians and hunting companions, and preying upon those that were too fearful or too aggressive to be around people. According to this view, humans purposefully altered the evolutionary path of the dog, transforming it from a predatory wolf-like creature into a preliminary version of the animal it is today.

Once the dog was destined to coexist with people, the process of domestication was further refined to selectively breed for certain traits. Domesticated animals are able to tolerate confinement and handling without becoming excessively stressed. In contrast to the wolf, dogs are less wary of new things and more easily socialized with people. But there are many other behavioural and physical differences. Dogs bark, they have a disproportionately smaller brain and smaller teeth, and they are inefficient predators. According to Coppinger, most dogs do not possess all the elements of hunting (eye, stalk, chase, bite) necessary to survive as predators. Did the early hominids desire a small-brained, yappy animal with tiny teeth and the inability to hunt, or did these changes happen by accident?

As it turns out, breeding for certain traits often leads to unrelated and unexpected changes. The Russian scientist Belyaev systematically mated silver foxes that displayed tame behaviour toward their human caretakers. Within just 20 years, these foxes were easier to handle, more responsive to people and less afraid of new things. The foxes also developed dog-like traits, including barking, droopy ears and curly tails. Females were prone to come into estrus twice a year rather than just once and, most devastating to the research project, some of the foxes had black-and-white piebald coats! Scientists do not fully understand why these unrelated traits are genetically linked to tame behaviour in foxes, but it is likely that similar unexpected developments occurred during domestication of the dog.

The real "hidden life of dogs"

One of my favorite Gary Larson *Far Side* cartoons depicts a pack of perfectly coiffed poodles racing across the Serengeti. In some parts of the world, dogs do survive in a feral state, having little or no contact with humans. How do dogs behave when they are left to their own devices?

Elizabeth Marshall Thomas describes in her book, *The Hidden Life of Dogs*, how she permitted her dog to roam freely in an urban environment to learn what dogs do there. Italian scientist Dr. Luigi Boitani and his research colleagues opted for a more rigorous, and safer, approach. Their three-year observation of a population of feral dogs in the mountainous Abruzzo region of central Italy provides us with a glimpse into the beast within our domestic pets. 'Wild' dog society consisted of loose social groups of three to six unrelated adults. Males were overrepresented in the groups because females were likely to be killed by the villagers in an effort to curb reproduction. Relations among the dogs within a group were amicable.

The village dumps offered an unlimited source of food for the dogs, including slaughterhouse refuse. Researchers never saw the dogs preying on livestock or wild animals. The dogs occasionally chased hares and squirrels, but the activity seemed to be more playful than predatory. Dogs were seen foraging on carcasses of livestock and wild boar that died from other causes.

These groups of feral dogs defended territories about two hectares in size and rarely ventured outside these areas. Aggression between groups was observed primarily at the dump. Even there, actual fighting was uncommon; instead groups barked at each other until one group chased the other off. Members within a group worked together to fend off other competitors, such as wolves. Aside from these hostile encounters, dogs and wolves did not appear to interact.

Females came into estrus about once every seven to eight months and all mature females in a group bores litters. Permanent bonds between individual males and females were not formed—mating was promiscuous. Unlike all other *canid* species, the feral dog males did not participate in care of the young and the dams were on their own when raising their puppies. Litters averaged between three to six puppies. Pup survival rates were extremely low, with 70% of the puppies dying within the first 70 days. Most pups succumbed when they started leaving the den site at two to three months of age, although the researchers were rarely able to discern an exact cause of death. Only five percent of the puppies born during the study period survived beyond one year of age. None of the groups produced enough offspring to replace losses due to mortality. Groups maintained their size, not by reproduction, but by joining up with stray village dogs.

The beast within

Boitani's study confirms that dogs are scavengers, not hunters. They don't require our companionship, but they do need our garbage! And dogs need our care to be able to thrive and reproduce in numbers sufficient to replace themselves. We may never know for sure whether our ancestors set out to tame the dog for specific purposes or if the dog chose us as the ticket to a free lunch, but dogs are certainly one of the most successful species on earth. As Coppinger points out, there are a zillion dogs out there, lounging on comfortable sofas and eating prime foods, while their human owners slog off to work each day to earn sufficient money to keep their pampered pets in rawhide. I would say they've done quite well for themselves!

DOGS AT PLAY

How Adult Canines Can Benefit From This Social Interaction

The two dogs chased each other around and around the clearing. Occasionally, Micky stopped and bowed to Tess, his play partner, and then took off again in another direction. Both dogs were completely enjoying the game. Eventually, Micky tuckered out and lay down, his huge tongue dangling several inches out of his mouth! Tess joined him and the two friends rolled around, gently biting at each other. For sure, it's a dog's life.

Dogs are unusual among mammals because they play throughout adulthood. Virtually all mammals and some birds play as youngsters. When animals mature, the amount of time they spend playing drops dramatically. Dogs may be an exception because we've genetically selected them to exhibit infantile behaviour.

Dogs show two distinct types of play. Social play occurs between two or more animals and can take the form of chase games, wrestling, and mouth sparring. Object play occurs between a dog and a toy, such as a stick or a tennis ball. Some dogs prefer object play, some prefer social play, and still others engage in social play but with an object as the focus of attention.

The function of play
Why do dogs play? Believe it or not, we really don't know. Play has received limited study by scientists but they've proposed several ideas for why animals play.

Play to establish social rank

One popular theory is that animals engage in play as a way to establish social rank, or dominance status, without fighting. Play fighting enables a dog to learn a great deal about the capabilities of his opponent—his strength, agility, fighting prowess, and desire to win. This valuable information can be acquired in a safe interchange and filed away for later. Rarely is real fighting necessary.

This theory has been questioned in part because partners sometimes reverse their social roles in play. High status dogs have been observed to do what has been termed self-handicapping—they assume a subordinate position and allow the play partner to dominate them even though they hold a higher rank. This is often observed when an adult dog plays with a young puppy—the adult lies on his back and allows the puppy to bite him. However, recent studies of dog play paint a different picture and now it's unclear whether dogs actually do reverse roles and self-handicap. More often than not, when two dogs play together repeatedly, one dog always prefers to be the top wrestler or chaser, while the other ends up on the bottom or being chased. While play is undoubtedly a complex, choreographed exchange between players, we don't yet understand how the game affects the overall political landscape.

Play as practice

Yet another notion is that play allows animals to hone behaviours for use later. Young dogs are able to growl, stand over, bite, and scruff-shake opponents. These are skills an adult dog needs in order to function in a social group. Ideally, the dog gets a chance to become comfortable with these skills *before* he finds himself in a situation where he needs them. Some courtship and mating behaviours also appear in play, long before an animal would actually use the behaviours in their 'real' context.

Other behaviours involved in play are seen during hunting—dogs stalk, chase, pounce on, and even bring down playmates. Presumably, a hunter is going to be more effective if he's had the opportunity to rehearse hunting skills before he has to face his first live meal. It's well established that mother cats bring home prey so their kittens can practice their hunting and killing skills from a young age. Mother canids don't do this for their pups, so play may be their only rehearsal stage.

Play when there's nothing else to do

Others think that play has no function at all. Instead, play is merely a default activity that animals engage in for enjoyment when there's nothing else to do. Domestic dogs play simply because they don't have to spend time hunting, mating, and resting. This is consistent with the fact that wolves spend a substantial amount of time playing when they live in captivity, but rarely do so in the wild—typically only when youngsters are present.

Play to develop intellect

An innovative idea is that play provides a vehicle for developing cognitive skills, such as abstraction, deceit and make-believe. Dogs that spend a lot of time playing are believed to be more adept at 'reading' and communicating with others and have learned how to 'lie,' which is a beneficial skill for a competitive social animal. Research with baboons has shown that dominant animals are better than subordinates at sending and receiving communication signals. Not only do they read other animals better but they are confident in their ability to function in a social environment and process social information more effectively. The extent to which this occurs in dogs is as yet unknown.

How do dogs communicate a desire to play?

Most, if not all, of the behaviours displayed during play also appear during hunting, fighting, socializing and mating. How does a dog know that a bite during play is not the same as a bite during aggression? It appears that dogs give 'play signals' to communicate, "What I'm going to do next is play, so don't get upset when I bite you." The most familiar dog play signal is the play bow (lowering the forequarters while maintaining an upright stance in the rear). Dogs are most likely to give a play bow to get play started or to re-start if the playmate gets distracted.

Dr. Erich Klinghammer, of Wolf Park in Indiana, disputes that the bow is a signal solely reserved for play. Several years ago, my Saluki and I visited Wolf Park. Dr. Klinghammer had recently acquired a herd of bison and he proposed that we release Shaahiin into the field to see what would happen. Thinking this would be a dream-come-true for Shaahiin, I agreed. Shaahiin ran at the bison, but, unlike rabbits and squirrels, they did not flee, and Shaahiin instantly dropped into a play bow. Why? Dr. Klinghammer thinks that the bow is actually very useful for canids hunting large prey. It allows the dog to quickly accelerate in any direction, which is particularly helpful if the prey is just as likely to charge you as it is to run away. Dogs no doubt retain this behaviour from their wolf ancestors who preyed upon large animals such as bison and elk.

Is play important for dogs?

Dogs seem to get great pleasure from playing. Owners should provide play opportunities right from day one. Good puppy kindergarten classes include play sessions to ensure the puppies keep their social skills sharpened, now that they are no longer with littermates and Mom. The best classes also teach the owners how to play interactively with their puppies.

Dogs that are taken to a park everyday to play with other dogs and their owners are usually better behaved at home. Play provides mental and physical stimulation and, because of the regular contact with other dogs and people, fear and aggression problems are rare. In general, play may be the best antidote for the prevention of behaviour problems and, at the same time, play improves the quality of life for both dogs and their owners.

The Play's The Thing

But It's Important to Know that Humans and Dogs Play Differently

---

During puppy classes, I used to include an exercise called the tail-wagging contest. I'd pair two puppies and their owners against each other. Each owner was instructed to play with his or her puppy with the goal of having the pup wag its tail as vigorously as possible. A panel of judges (classmates) watched the teams and clapped for the pair they felt was having the most fun. We continued until we had an ultimate tail-wagger!

Sounds easy, right? Well, I'm sad to report that I eventually gave up on this contest because it broke my heart to see how many people were unable to play with their puppies.

Some puppies acted afraid of their owners' antics, others simply ignored the owner and watched the other puppies, and still others stared at their owner like they'd never seen them before! I decided it was necessary to actually teach people how to play.

"I want to play!"

Believe it or not, behavioural scientists have actually studied the dynamics of play between dogs and people. Play between people is very different from play between dogs. Dogs bark and run, jump and bite. People prefer to smile and laugh, tickle and wrestle. How do the two species even manage to play with each other?

Researchers from the University of Southampton in the U.K. observed owners playing with their dogs at home. They were especially interested in watching for signals used by the participants to spark play. Dogs use a specific signal, called the play bow (elbows on the ground, butt in the air), to let other dogs know that subsequent behaviours are playful. The play bow conveys important information because play contains a lot of aggressive behaviours. The use of the play bow avoids misunderstandings that could lead to fights and injuries.

People also have a specific signal for play that we share with other primates: the play face. When we invite play, we open our eyes wide and display a broad open mouth with our lips pulled back to expose our teeth. However, when owners invite their dogs to play they are most likely to pat the floor. Other common signals were whispers, claps, and motions to shove the dog away.

Once play was underway, both dogs and owners engaged in what appeared to be aggressive looking behaviour. Dogs growled, jumped, and mouthed at their owners. Owners hit, kicked, pushed, and poked at their dogs. How does each player know that the other is just playing?

Like play between dogs, clear play signals in the beginning stages of the interaction guarantee that neither party falls prey to a misunderstanding. The pats, claps and shoves given by the owner to invite play from the dog appear to let the dog know that the owner is not angry with the dog when play escalates to hits and kicks.

Familiarity breeds play

Psychologist Robert Mitchell at Eastern Kentucky University examined play between dogs and humans as a function of how well the dog knows the person. Dr. Mitchell observed owners playing with their own dogs and playing with an unfamiliar dog. Not only were dogs more willing to play with their owners than with strangers, the types of games played differed. In fact, familiar play partners were especially prone to 'fooling' each other in play. Both dogs and people enjoyed playing catch-me-if-you-can: come close and then dodge out of reach at the last second. Owners faked their dogs out by pretending to throw toys and by making a toy available to the dog but snatching it away before the dog could reach it. This playful deception was much less common between dogs and unfamiliar people.

Puppy play

The problem I witnessed most often in my classes was that owners were too overbearing when playing with their puppies. They ran, they jumped, they loomed, and they wrestled. Some puppies liked this right away but most need to build up to this intensity. Young puppies play well with wiggling fingers, toes, and soft toys. Once the puppy learns to recognize people play—which can take as little as a few minutes—the play can be more vigorous. As the puppy develops physically and mentally, play becomes erratic and rough.

The two games I encouraged my students to play with their dogs were chase and tug. Chase games establish the foundation for a great Recall. Dogs love to chase and they love to be chased.

Entice your puppy to chase you: hold him at arm's length, get him excited with your voice ("Are you ready?!") and then take off, calling his name! When he catches you, reward him with a quick bout of you chasing him. He'll find it hard to resist coming after you whenever he sees you run. Run away from him frequently, always calling his name as you take off. Sometimes, when he catches you, deke off in another direction. Or wave a toy in his face and let him grab it.

This can be done in the house, in the yard, at the park, everywhere. It won't take long before the dog is checking in with you all the time, just in case you might feel the urge for a game of chase. Dogs that have learned this game are not only extremely attentive to their owners' whereabouts, but they are also very responsive to their own name.

Tug-of-war is another valuable game to play with a puppy because it contributes to the formation of a close bond between dog and owner. Games like fetch teach the dog to have fun *away* from the owner; tug teaches the dog to *come to* the owner to have fun. Of course, it is necessary to teach the puppy to release the toy on cue so the owner controls the game. I use the opportunity for more tugging as the reward for releasing the toy. This results in a dramatically fast response when I say "Give" to my dogs. They practically spit the toy out at me! I then add a sit into the sequence so the dog automatically sits in anticipation of being offered the toy again. It gives an owner tremendous confidence to be able to wind their dog up to the height of wild excitement and, with a simple word like "give," have a dog sitting at their feet. What an off switch! And, contrary to popular belief, playing tug with a dog does not encourage aggressive behaviour. At least three scientific studies have found no connection between aggression and activities like tug-of-war.

If your puppy or dog is reluctant to tug, try a variety of toys. Some dogs like rope toys; others find them too hard. My dogs' favorite tug toys are Crash Test toys (www.pathcom.com/~crasher/). You can choose between fake and 'politically correct' real fur made from re-cycled fur coats purchased at Goodwill. These toys are very chewable so it's important to put them away when you are not actively playing with your dog.

Cautious players

Some dogs never learned to play as puppies and they can often be a hard sell. I once adopted a Saluki as a mature adult and she didn't know how to play with people or with dogs. When she was really ex-cited watching other dogs play, she would mount one of the playing dogs and hang on for dear life. I knew it was a major breakthrough the first time she tried this with me! Needless to say, once she loos-ened up like this, I took the opportunity to teach her more accept-able ways to play.

Some dogs don't respond to the usual sorts of play. As a puppy, Eejit, didn't want to chase a thrown ball but he really turned on when I tried kicking it. Now I use a quick game of soccer to reward him for even the slightest offer to chase the ball first. His interest in a kicked ball has now generalized to anything that I kick, including leaves and snow. My older dog was the same way as a puppy and now we enjoy a game called "feet." I kick my foot and he leaps straight up in the air!

It has evolved into a bizarre-looking routine that I use to warm him up before we go into the agility ring. Best of all, I don't need toys so we can play anytime, anywhere.

Release your dog's inner puppy

Ninety-five percent of pet owners consider their dogs friends. Play is an essential part of this friendship for most owners. Dogs love to play, even into adulthood. Dogs give people an outlet for their own playfulness, allowing us to let loose and act silly. Play also reminds both dogs and owners that training and hanging out together should be fun.

The benefits of play with dogs are immeasurable. Make sure you encourage your dog to regularly release his "inner puppy!"

CALMING SIGNALS

Body Language and Behaviour Can Pacify a Stressed Dog

Spike, an 18-month-old male Vizsla, and his owner, Samantha, entered the church basement to attend their first obedience class. They passed a Dalmatian that barked and rushed at them, but fortunately the Dalmatian's owner had a firm hold of the leash. Spike and Sam were out of reach. They headed for the corner. Spike shifted closer to his owner, licked his lips, and gave an exaggerated yawn as he scanned the room.

The class instructor looked up, grabbed her clipboard and walked toward the new duo. Spike watched as she approached. As she got closer, he pulled his ears back against his head, shifted most of his weight to his hind legs, and began to pant. The instructor looked directly at Spike, reached her hand out to him and exclaimed, "Welcome! What a beautiful dog you have!" Before she even had a chance to see Spike's bit of tucked tail, he barked and lunged straight up in the direction of her face. Spike's owner screamed and pulled back on the leash. Thankfully, Spike didn't make contact and no harm was done. But how could this reaction from Spike have been prevented?

Signs of stress and arousal

Did Spike provide any signals to indicate how he was feeling prior to lunging? Could the instructor have guessed that Spike was stressed and aroused in this new situation? When moderately stressed, most dogs will show signs. The dog might have a wide-eyed expression, laid-back ears, dilated pupils, or he might lick his lips, yawn, and tuck his tail. As he becomes more anxious, he may begin to pant, whine, salivate profusely, pace, stiffen, try to escape, or become aggressive. In Spike's case, he was moderately stressed from being in a novel and chaotic environment, and then he became highly stressed when the instructor invaded his 'flight zone.' When animals are frightened and unable to flee, they sometimes resort to aggression.

Reducing anxiety

If the instructor had been more observant, she would have recognized some of these signals in Spike's behaviour. But could she have changed the way Spike was feeling by behaving differently herself?

Observations of the way dogs behave towards each other in similar situations suggest that she could. My young dog demonstrates this beautifully. As he approaches an unfamiliar dog, he averts his gaze toward the ground, hunches his back, and flips upside down right underneath the dog's face. The human translation? "I am friendly. I am completely non-threatening. I want to say hello and perhaps play." The great majority of dogs, even ones known to be aggressive toward other dogs, respond positively to this greeting.

Now don't get me wrong—I'm not suggesting the instructor should have turned upside down in front of Spike! But dogs do seem to recognize the same sort of message from a person who averts her gaze, approaches slowly and at an angle (naturally slow, though, not the stilted motion of a stalking cat), and adopts a low, crouching position in front of the dog. Perhaps if the instructor had done this, Spike would have backed away from her, then given her a tentative sniff and, finally, moved closer to investigate this non-threatening stranger.

Scientists who study animal communication call this a submissive display. The purpose of a display is to convey your intentions to the other animal. The instructor, quite inadvertently, communicated a more assertive and intimidating message to Spike—she approached directly, looked straight at him and reached out her hand. Spike read this message to mean, "I think I am stronger than you; I may be dangerous."

Calming signals

In her book *On Talking Terms With Dogs* Turid Rugaas, a dog trainer from Norway, uses the term "calming signals" to describe behaviours a person should display when dealing with a stressed animal like Spike. She recommends reacting immediately to the first indications of stress. I whole-heartedly aggress with Rugaas on this point. People who work with dogs must be able to recognize signs of stress and take immediate action to reduce pressure on the dog. If the stress is induced by the approach of a person or a dog, the appropriate response is to back off or modify the approach so as not to intimidate the dog.

Rugaas also interprets calming signals to include some of the dog's own indicators of stress, such as yawning, lip licking, and panting. Ethologists, most notably Konrad Lorenz, identified these behaviours as "displacement activities." Lorenz believed that these seemingly irrelevant behaviours appear when the dog is in a state of conflict between different motivations. In Spike's case, he probably felt as thought he'd like to flee from the situation but could not because he was leashed and forced to stay with his owner. Torn between staying and leaving, he displaced his energies into yawning and lip licking.

Rugaas feels that a dog engages in these behaviours as a way to reduce the stress he is experiencing. Subjectively, this seems to make good sense—in a stressful situation, I feel better when I bite my nails. By engaging in this behaviour, I can direct my attentions away from the source of my anxiety. However, Rugaas argues that a stressed dog that is licking his lips and yawning will relax if the source of his fear (for instance, a frightening person) also licks her lips and yawns. She feels that a person working with an anxious dog should mimic the dog's behaviour in order to reduce the dog's anxiety.

I find this notion puzzling. It doesn't fit with my own human experience. I can't imagine feeling relaxed through seeing the people around me also biting their nails. That would tell me they are stressed as well. I'd probably become even more distressed and bite my nails with renewed vigor!

Fluency in dog language

Despite this weakness in Rugaas's theory of calming signals, she has focused our attention on a very important point. Those of us who share our lives with dogs need to become well versed in both reading and speaking 'dog.' We need to 'read' dog in order to recognize when our dog is uncomfortable in a situation. We need to identify the source of that discomfort and determine ways to alleviate the dog's anxiety.

If it's not an important issue, simply remove the dog from the situation. For instance, my dog became very anxious in the presence of a person dressed in a dog costume. I could have spent time and effort teaching him that people dressed up as dogs are not at all scary, but would have been worth it? How often would he see such a thing? I opted to remove him instead.

On the other hand, if he had shown the same reaction to a child, I would have made the effort to deal with the problem. I would determine what level of exposure to children he'd tolerate without anxiety and gradually build up his confidence.

We also need to 'speak' dog in order to know how best to behave around dogs ourselves. If I am meeting a nervous dog like Spike and I want him to feel comfortable in my presence, I need to be able to convey a message of friendliness and submission. If Spike had been greeted by an observant instructor, fluent in reading and speaking dog, his first night of obedience class would probably have been a much more positive experience.

MYTH BUSTERS

A Survey Dispels Some Common
Beliefs about Dog Behaviour

I wish I had a nickel for every time I've heard "Dogs smell fear and will bite you," "Playing tug-of-war makes a dog aggressive," "Dogs that sleep on the bed are dominant," or "My dog chews things up when he's mad at me." Beliefs about dog behaviour abound, but how do we separate truth from fiction?

I prefer to turn to science for substantiation of truth, but our lack of actual knowledge about dog behaviour is quite astonishing. Dogs are typically overlooked by scientists because they are domesticated and, therefore, considered 'artificial' animals.

Two behaviourists, Dr. Peter Borchelt, and Dr. Linda Goodloe, have taken a giant step toward rectifying this state of affairs. They embarked on a monumental project in which they surveyed over 2,000 American dog owners. Each owner took twenty to forty-five minutes to answer 127 questions about their dog's behaviour in a variety of contexts, such as, "Does your dog bark, whine, or howl when owner/family member leaves?" or "Has your dog bitten another dog?" For each question, the owner could choose one of five answers ranging from 1 (Never) to 5 (Always). Only owners of dogs over one year of age were eligible for the study.

I won't go into detail about how the researchers analyzed the results, but they basically looked for behaviours that occurred in combination. For instance, you might expect a dog that is aggressive to strangers on the street to also bark at guests in the home and to be nervous at the veterinary clinic. This type of analysis can also identify possible contributing factors. For example, maybe dogs that are aggressive to strangers are more likely to have suffered an illness during puppyhood that would have compromised the socialization process; or maybe these dogs experienced abuse at the hands of strangers.

Many of the survey findings were not surprising. For instance, dogs that howled when left alone were also likely to be distraught when the owners prepared to leave, were more likely to greet them enthusiastically upon their return, and followed family members about the house. However, the study did reveal several interesting correlations between behaviours, and some intriguing *lack of correlations* between other behaviours.

Three distinct types of aggression

A few weeks ago, I visited with a woman whose adult dog had killed their new puppy with one quick bite to the head. Her purpose in contacting me was not because she intended to introduce another puppy, but to address her concern that the dog would now become aggressive to her children or her cats. I often encounter this notion that aggression spreads like a virus. Owners believe that if the dog bites a guest, for example, it will become aggressive toward the children in the family, or a dog that is nasty to the cat will begin to terrorize people in the neighborhood.

The analysis of this survey made it evident that aggression is not a single, general trait. The researchers identified three independent categories of aggression, distinguished by the target to which the aggression is directed:

1. family members

2. strangers

3. other dogs.

There was a small tendency for dogs that are aggressive to strangers to also be aggressive toward dogs, presumably because some dogs are liable to show aggression toward anything unfamiliar, whether dogs or people.

The creation of a dictator

Aggression toward family members consists of a variety of behaviours that characterize what most behaviourists consider 'dominance aggression.' These dogs are likely to respond aggressively when handled or disciplined and are apt to guard objects, such as food and toys. There are plenty of myths about activities that contribute to the expression of dominance aggression—everything from playing tug with the dog to letting the dog sleep on the bed to feeding the dog before the family eats.

Here's one of the most noteworthy results of this study. Dogs that enjoy tug-of-war or rough play with people are *no more likely* to show dominance aggression than dogs that do not. This will come as no surprise to the many dog trainers who frequently play tug as a reward for their dogs. However, it always amazes me that these same professionals will advise pet owners not to play tug with their dogs for fear of encouraging aggression.

Yet another revelation is that sharing your bed with a dog has no association with dominance aggression. This is not to say that dogs showing dominance aggression will not become aggressive on the bed—guarding resources, including resting places, can be a manifestation of a dominance-subordinance relationship. What this does mean is that permitting your dog to sleep on the bed will not lead him to become aggressive.

Mounting behaviour is also assumed to be an expression of dominance but, according to this study, a dog that attempts to mount family members is not prone to aggression. This supports my assertion that dogs will mount for a variety of reasons, including play, arousal, and just plain pleasure.

According to the study, males, whether intact or castrated, are more likely to display dominance aggression than females. However, males that show 'male-related' behaviours, such as frequent urine-marking, raising the leg during urination, and excessive sniffing during walks, are not necessarily prone to aggression. Consistent with other studies, the survey revealed that spayed females are more likely to be aggressive to family members than are intact females. It may come as a surprise to many, but young females showing tendencies toward dominance aggression should not be spayed until the problem is resolved, as spaying removes the 'non-aggressive' influences of the female reproductive hormones.

The makings of a serial killer

Play is often considered to be 'practice' for hunting and I sometimes hear owners say that they don't encourage their dogs to play with stuffed animals or furry toys because they fear the dog will go on to kill small animals. I always recount the day my two experienced lure-coursing Salukis who spied a tiny Maltese sprinting approximately two football fields away. They took off in hot pursuit but broke off their pursuits after only about one hundred yards, recognizing that this was *not* a bunny. The survey showed that predation in pet dogs is a very rare occurrence and there was no correlation whatsoever between predation and play behaviours, such as chasing moving objects, vigorously shaking toys, or carrying objects in the mouth. Predatory play does not make a dog more inclined to become a killer of small animals.

The impact of obedience training

Is obedience training a general panacea for problem dogs? Despite findings to the contrary from other studies, this survey confirmed that the amount of obedience training received by the dog and owner does relate to more desirable behaviours. Dogs with obedience training are less likely to be aggressive to people, destructive or suffer from separation anxiety, and are more likely to be playful, friendly, and compliant. I found it interesting to note that aggression toward dogs is the one form of aggression that showed no link to the extent of obedience training the dog received.

Be aware that we can't know, from this result alone, that obedience training has a direct effect on the prevention of behaviour problems. It may simply be that owners who take their dogs for obedience training are more likely to spend time with their dogs, socialize their dogs more, or have more realistic expectations of their dogs than other owners.

Myth busters

The value of this survey is that we now have a clearer idea of what activities are *not* associated with problem behaviours. The unfortunate thing is that we still don't know what things *do* predispose a dog to specific problems. I suspect this is because the contributing factors are so complex, resulting from an interplay between the dog's genetic makeup, the dog's experiences, and the dog's relationship with the owner.

There are no easy answers. With this study, as with science in general, the quest for truth leads to more questions. Chipping away at our foundation of beliefs enables us to construct a road of knowledge, busting myths along the way.

THE COMPLEXITY OF PACK LIFE
Coping With and Managing Multi-dog Households

You stand in the doorway of your house, waving, as your precious puppy watches out the car window, nestled in the arms of her new owner. You met this couple fourteen years ago when they purchased their first puppy from you. They provided a wonderful home for the now elderly dog and the main question on their minds as they leave is, "How will she respond to this new addition?"

Living with multiple dogs is a completely different experience from living with only one. The dogs form special relationships among themselves and they display a wealth of fascinating social behaviour that you might never see from a solitary dog. More often than not, the behaviour is amicable, but every now and then, conflict can erupt.

Introducing a new puppy to the pack
Generally, adult dogs are typically quite tolerant of puppies. The wolf—a close relative to the dog—lives in small social groups and all the adults become involved in raising and caring for the pups. The pups enjoy liberties that they would never get away with as adults. They romp around and over the grown-ups, they nibble at Mom's flicking ears, they leap on the big male's head or pull his tail, and the most they incur is a growl or snap. This 'puppy privilege' enables many people to introduce a new pup to their existing pack with little

upheaval. Except for the odd scolding, the pup gets away with being a brat for the first few months and by the time adolescence hits, the newcomer is an established part of the gang.

There are some adult dogs who don't abide by the usual rules. They quite like other dogs, but *puppies*? That's a different kettle of fish entirely. Even these 'old codgers' rarely injure a puppy, but they often leave the poor tyke hiding in a corner, afraid to move. Such an environment is obviously damaging to the puppy's confidence and extra effort must be made to minimize uncontrolled interactions between the adult and the youngster. The puppy should have plenty of opportunity to meet friendly adult dogs so that he doesn't lose his social skills and become afraid of all dogs.

Unfortunately, some adult dogs actually do cause harm to puppies. While being managed carefully, these dogs need to learn that being around puppies is in their best interest. When I brought Eejit home as a pup, my six-year-old Border Collie was not at all impressed. Ciaran was very intolerant of puppies anyway—during his life, he had actually inflicted puncture wounds on two puppies that belonged to other people. He was so disturbed about this new puppy that he went to bed in the middle of the afternoon! When it was bedtime for all of us, including the puppy, he left the bedroom and slept elsewhere. I didn't have to worry about him hurting the youngster because he wouldn't go near him! However, within a couple of days, he recognized that with the puppy came toys. And, miraculously, I would play with him too! This was very special for him because— normally we didn't permit him access to toys in the house as he'd nag us to play all the time. So because of the extra access to toys, he and the newcomer became the best of friends!

Introducing an adult to the pack

Introducing an adult dog into a pre-existing pack can present some interesting challenges. On the one hand, they don't enjoy puppy status so full-blown fighting can ensue. On the other, an adult dog coming into a pack's territory tends to be rather subdued so as not to call attention to himself. He's well versed in canine communication signals and he knows he's in a treacherous situation. Conflicts can be kept to a minimum by introducing the newcomer to the pack

on neutral territory, so no one need feel threatened. Plan a get ac-
quainted party at the local park—lots of play and treats and toys.
Take a long walk as a group. After a couple of hours, everyone will be
quite relaxed with each other. Walk home together and let the new
dog enter the house first. In most cases, this will result in relative
harmony right from the start.

For the first few weeks, avoid potentially volatile situations. Keep
mealtimes and chew times controlled. Give each dog plenty of space
around his food bowl and don't allow them to switch bowls or lick
the empty bowls. Don't leave toys and leftover chewies lying around.
Crate the new dog during your absences so he doesn't get into trouble when the group rushes to meet you at the door. Teach each dog
to go through the door to the yard only when they hear their name
called, thus preventing the group from charging the door en masse.
And don't have the group loose in tightly confined places, like the
car. Take these precautions until you are very comfortable with the
group dynamics.

Resolving conflict

Sadly, an introduction may not proceed smoothly and the once-
peaceful group becomes fraught with squabbles and full blown argu-
ments. Even more disturbing is when two buddies that always got
along well suddenly become mortal enemies. I once met a breeder who had two young males, aged within a month of each other,
who had grown up as best buddies. One matured earlier than the
other and went off every weekend with his handler. Each reunion
was a jubilant affair. Then the day came when the younger boy was
considered ready and he was sent to the grooming salon. Upon his
return, amidst the "oohing" and "ahhing" of his human family, he
was viciously attacked by his pal. After that fight, they couldn't be
together—they bristled at each other on sight.

The best strategy for a problem like this is to keep the dogs apart. *Do
not* allow them to fight it out! While it's true that sometimes they can
work it out by fighting, the risk of injury is far too great. Sometimes
the dogs become even more antagonistic after a serious fight—they
anticipate further fighting and become defensive. With each dog acting like he's walking on eggshells, the chance of another fight erupt-

ing is high. After giving the dogs a few days to calm down, bring them together for short, fun sessions. Make sure you have helpers to keep both dogs occupied simultaneously. If fighting is likely, keep them tethered where they can see each other but not make contact. Hand out lots of treats, attention, and yummy things to chew. After each session, remove the dogs and ignore them—they will come to learn that when they are in each other's presence, they get your attention and lots of goodies. Gradually move them closer together. When you're ready to let them interact again, go for a long walk, each with their own handler, where they can sniff the smells, pee on a tree, say hi to passersby, and get re-acquainted without each being the centre of the other's attention. If all goes well, bring them home together, but be sure that you have removed all toys and chew bones so there's nothing to spark a conflict. Hand out lots of treats for good behaviour and interrupt the dogs immediately should they start posturing or threatening each other (shouting "squirrel" and running to the backyard can prove an irresistible distraction).

There are instances where the dogs never become friends again. Like people, some dogs are simply not compatible roommates. When this happens among wolves, one of the animals will emigrate from the group. If it's breaking the owner's heart to consider re-homing one of the dogs, it may help to explain how dispersal is a normal part of animal behaviour and that the dog will very likely be just fine in a different group. It's usually best for the youngest dog to go.

Hedging your bets

If you follow some basic guidelines, you can minimize the potential for discord in your canine pack. Mixing males and females is the best group composition, especially if they are spayed and neutered. However, some males will simply not tolerate another male in the group, even if they are neutered. If you have reproductively intact animals, you'll need to be watchful any time a female starts coming into estrous. Not only might you end up with an unwanted breeding, but the hormonal changes may trigger competition between males or intimidation of the bitch in heat by other females.

If you like having dogs of the same sex, neutered males are more likely to squabble than are spayed females; however, when females fight they are more likely to inflict injury. And there's some suggestion that females may be less likely to get along after a serious fight than males. Introducing a puppy into an existing group is almost always smoother than adding an adult to the pack. If you already have a playful adolescent dog, adding another teenager is your best bet.

Many people who become enamoured with dogs just can't stop with one. Two easily leads to three and on it goes. If you find yourself in a home with more dogs than people, sit back and enjoy the unique experiences that come with living in a canine pack!

THE DOG'S MIND

Canine Intellect is Surprising

A huge challenge faced by psychological science is to discover the workings of the mind. The human mind is mysterious enough; imagine trying to puzzle through an animal's mind when they are unable to relate their experiences to us. The investigation of mental activity in animals is a relatively new and fascinating science. We are just beginning to understand how animals deal with information—for instance, how they perceive other animals in their world, how they store and retrieve material from memory, how they judge the passage of time, and how they make inferences.

Until recently, dogs were rarely subjects of choice for psychological experiments because they are expensive to keep and they live a long time. Also, because they are domesticated, scientists consider them an 'artificial' species. However, dogs are being featured in animal cognition research these days, in part because of their history of coexistence with humans. So, while our knowledge of canine cognition is limited, we are attaining an occasional glimpse into the capabilities of the dog's mind.

Out of sight, out of mind?

Generations of humans have used dogs for hunting. Useful dogs keep hunting even if they can't always keep the prey in sight. This requires the capacity to understand that things exist even if they are not in view. Jean Piaget studied the development of mental abilities in humans and determined that children aged eighteen to twenty-four months gradually begin to grasp that when an object disappears from sight, it still exists. Prior to this age, children lack the concept of object permanence.

A group of researchers at Université Laval in Quebec decided to examine the extent of the dog's understanding of object permanence. They performed a test that involved attracting the dog's attention to a toy suspended on a string. Once the dog sighted the toy, the toy was moved behind one of three identical screens. The dog was then released to search for the toy. Numerous controls were in place to ensure the dog didn't simply smell where the toy was hidden. Adult dogs had no problem solving this visible displacement task. However, puppies did not comprehend where the toy was hidden until they were eight weeks old.

An invisible displacement test was substantially more challenging to the dogs. In this test, the dog watched while the toy was placed in a container. The container was moved behind one of the screens, the toy was removed, and the container was brought back into the dog's view. The dog was shown the empty container. In order for the dog to know which screen to search behind, he has to infer that the toy was removed when the container was out of view. Although the dogs made plenty of errors performing this task, a rudimentary understanding of invisible displacement appears to develop in dogs sometime between nine and twelve months of age.

The dog's social mind

A predominant theoretical view in the study of animal cognition is that animals evolve mental abilities that help them in their daily lives. For instance, animals that live in groups are likely to benefit from the ability to 'read' others more than animals preferring a solitary existence. This skill is particularly handy if one member of the group has found food and others want to join in the feast. Scientists figure that if an animal has this capability, it should be able to follow the gaze of another animal looking to a source of food.

Various problems testing for the skill of gaze-following have been posed to animals, primarily primate species. Typically, an 'informant,' who could be a person or another monkey, indicates the location of hidden food by looking and/or pointing at one of two containers. Capuchin monkeys, orangutans and chimpanzees were unable to guess the location of the food unless the informant actually touched or sat beside the correct container. Dogs, on the other hand, were quite skillful at this. They were able to infer that a person pointing at a container meant they were likely to find food under that container.

The dogs in the study were also capable of sending signals to people about the location of food. Dogs that knew where the food was located but couldn't get to it made noises to attract people and then looked back and forth between the person and the food, as though 'showing' the person.

Another study was designed to examine whether dogs were sensitive to what people do and what their activities might mean for dogs. A researcher placed treats around the floor and told the dog not to touch the treats. The person stayed in the room, sat in a chair and either looked directly at the dog, played with a handheld computer game, closed their eyes or turned their back to the dog. The dogs stole twice as much food when the person was not looking directly at them. When the person was preoccupied with the game, the dog was quite blatant about stealing the food. If the person was keeping an eye on the dog, the dog wandered around the room, as though uninterested in the treats, and occasionally snatched one up!

Dog smarts

The study of canine cognition is in its infancy but already dogs have shown surprising intellect. It is commonly believed that domesticated species are mentally inferior to their wild counterparts, presumably because of their 'easy' life with humans. However, dogs' association with humans may have actually prompted the evolution of select cognitive skills that help them excel in our world. They appear to have flexible minds, capable of complex learning and problem-solving, and able to deal with reasonably sophisticated concepts. To be sure, there are many exciting questions about the canine mind waiting to be tackled but I'm confident that dogs will turn out to be pretty smart cookies!

2011 update

Oh, to be a graduate student in animal behaviour at this time! A tremendous amount of research has been conducted on canine cognition since I wrote this essay. In fact, it is one of the most rapidly-growing areas in the field of animal behaviour, with major dog cognition institutes in Austria, Hungary, and the United States. A summary of the work would now constitute an entire textbook. There have been studies on dogs' understanding of numbers, their skill at making inferences, their ability to find effective detours, their recognition of human faces and voices, and even their capacity to appreciate fairness, to name just a few areas of study. We're discovering that with regard to some tasks, dogs are surprisingly clever; but when faced with other tasks, they are spectacularly dense. More often than not, their strengths and weaknesses make sense when you consider the dogs' long affiliation with humans. Still the most prolific area of work is on dogs interpreting human gestures and how they have evolved cognitive skills enabling them to survive and thrive in a world dominated by humans. The coming years of research will reveal much more of what goes on in the mind of the dog.

DOGGY SEE, DOGGY DO

Are Animals Capable of Learning by Imitation?

Have you watched your dogs and wondered if they learn from each other? I've often had owners tell me that their puppy learned specific behaviours from their older dog. Psychologists have long been fascinated with the question of whether animals can imitate each other.

Researchers in South Africa raised litters of German Shepherd dogs with their dams until twelve weeks of age. One set of puppies was present while their dams practiced their narcotics search-and-retrieve skills. The other group of puppies was not afforded this opportunity. At six months of age, each puppy's aptitude for search work was assessed. The puppies that watched their moms performing scored significantly higher than the naïve pups. Did these puppies learn what to do by watching or is something else going on?

What is social learning?

Social learning is a broad term that encompasses any situation in which one animal's behaviour is influenced by the presence of another. Scientists are sticklers for using precise terms. It may seem to the uninitiated that psychologists go overboard with jargon, but when it comes to the issue of social learning, there is a need for clarity. What does it mean to say that one animal learns from another? When one dog learns to eat a particular type of food because he is surrounded by other dogs that eat the food, is this imitation? How about when one dog watches another perform a complex behaviour, like heeling, and picks it up more quickly than would be expected? It turns out that psychologists have identified three very distinct forms of social learning: social facilitation; stimulus enhancement; and imitation.

Social facilitation: Getting lost in the crowd

Social facilitation is the simplest form of social learning. It is often used to describe 'mob behaviour,' where one animal tends to do what everyone else is doing. For instance, you can give a dog all the food he wishes to eat until he's satiated, then place him with other dogs chowing down and he will eat even more. It has long been recognized that people in crowds will engage in certain behaviours, such as looting, that they would never dream of doing if alone.

You can rightly argue that these examples do not involve learning—the dog already knew how to eat and the person may never steal again. Learning can result, though, if the person or animal performs the behaviour in new circumstances.

Let me describe a very clever study on socially facilitated learning. Starlings often fall prey to owls and, if an owl is detected nearby, the bird will give an alarm call to warn others. A researcher designed a cage that held two starlings—a demonstrator and an observer—in separate compartments. The observer starling could see two things from his compartment: the demonstrator and a Coke bottle. The demonstrator could see a stuffed owl. Upon seeing the owl, the demonstrator began flapping around and alarm calling. The observer bird also started alarm calling but all it could see was the Coke bottle. In subsequent sessions, the observer bird showed that it had learned to fear Coke bottles!

Years ago, when our Saluki, Shaahiin, was a youngster, he flatly refused to eat dry dog cookies. Then we fostered a Saluki that loved cookies! Shaahiin watched Cassandra gobble up cookies for a few days before he was inspired to try one. He learned to like them because he continued to eat cookies even after Cassandra left for her new home and Shaahiin was on his own again. He was socially facilitated to try the cookies and this experience led to new learning on his part.

I suspect many young dogs become house-trained through the process of social facilitation. They accompany the adult dogs to their favourite areas of the yard, everyone else is urinating so they do too; quickly, they learn to seek out these areas when they feel the need to eliminate.

Stimulus enhancement: Check this out!

Stimulus enhancement, or goal emulation, describes a situation where one animal observes another engaging in a behaviour in a specific location or with a specific object and is inspired to check things himself. For instance, one dog watches another dog operate the pedal of a lidded garbage can and score some goodies. As a result of this observation, the dog is prompted to investigate the garbage can, making it more likely that he learns, by trial and error, to step on the pedal and open the lid. So the observer doesn't learn to copy the demonstrator's behaviour per se, he simply learns that the garbage can is something worth investigating.

You might suppose the same thing could happen if aliens came to earth and watched us all troop up to the ATM machines, get money, and go buy food! The aliens would be drawn to the machines, but they'd still have to figure out how to key in the correct information. I liken this to the experience I had when I was compelled to mow the lawn so I could find my agility equipment buried in the grass. I had never used our new tractor lawn mower; I had watched my husband Nick use the mower a few times, but it didn't help me at all when I wanted to use it and Nick wasn't home. I knew the machine would do the trick if I could just get it going, but I had to learn by trial and error how to start and drive it!

A naturally occurring example of stimulus enhancement was documented in England when people in certain regions began complaining that someone was pilfering the cream off their bottled milk. The milkman would deliver a perfectly intact bottle of milk, complete with cream on top, but, by the time the family retrieved it from the doorstep, someone had pierced the top and skimmed off all the tasty cream. As it turned out, the culprit was a species of bird called the blue tit, a cousin of our black-capped chickadees. The thieving occurred only in certain regions because the birds were learning from each other, through stimulus enhancement.

A researcher at the University of Toronto simulated this scenario in his laboratory. He taught certain chickadees to pull off the tops of small restaurant creamers to gain access to tasty seeds. He permitted other chickadees to watch. When he gave the observers creamers in their own cage, they were no faster at learning to open them than were the chickadees that just watched others eating from already-opened creamers. In other words, they didn't learn by watching how to open the cream tubs, they simply learned that these tubs contained something good to eat.

One of my dogs learned to operate a doggy gumball machine in this manner. I taught the older dog to push the lever with his paw. The young dog watched him get all these goodies, eventually pushed him out of the way, and bit, chewed, and barked at the thing! It took a bit of time but he eventually figured out how to operate it on his own.

True imitation: The ultimate form of learning

Imitation occurs when one animal watches another perform a *novel* behaviour and, as a result of this observation, the animal is able to mimic the new behaviour. People imitate all the time. Children learn to tie their shoelaces by watching their parents demonstrate the procedure. Aspiring dancers watch the instructor's feet and copy the moves. Dog owners observe the skill of their trainer and attempt to repeat the same movements themselves. When I wasn't able to figure out the lawnmower, I watched carefully while Nick started and operated it, then I copied him. Imitation is an extremely efficient form of learning.

The evidence for animals showing imitative learning is not very convincing. First, it is very difficult to actually design an experiment that adequately rules out stimulus enhancement and social facilitation.

Imagine this scenario, called the "two-action test." You have an apparatus that delivers food. It can be operated either by depressing a lever with a paw or by pushing a bar with a nose. One group of dogs watches a demonstrator depressing with his paw. Another group of dogs watches a demonstrator pushing with his nose. Both groups of dogs see the demonstrator manipulating the same apparatus to get food so the impact of stimulus enhancement is the same for both groups. When you give the observers access to the apparatus, do the ones who watched the paw behaviour use their paw and do the ones who watched the nose behaviour use their nose? If you documented that the one group of dogs mimicked the pawing behaviour and the other group mimicked the nosing behaviour, you would convince most scientists that dogs can imitate.

While this experiment has never been done with dogs (it would be an excellent graduate thesis for someone out there!), similar studies have been done with a variety of other species and the findings are inconclusive. Only chimpanzees and orangutans come close to the imitative capacities of human children, but parrots, rats, pigeons and quail have shown some skill at imitating others. Without further study, we know that dogs are very capable of learning by social facilitation and stimulus enhancement, but they may well draw the line at imitation.

What about the German Shepherd pups?

I suspect some readers will not be convinced because they have seen their dogs do something that certainly looks like imitation. I ask you first to reconsider the example from the start of this essay and see if you can't account for it through social facilitation or stimulus enhancement.

A critical look at the study with the GSD puppies generated two alternative explanations. First, the researchers reported that, although the pups had no direct exposure to the sachets of narcotics, they often jumped up to nuzzle the dam's mouth as she carried the object. It is well established that the young of many species display clear preferences for the types of food eaten by their mothers—information that is gleaned by sniffing the mother's mouth. It is possible that the observer pups were more attracted to the narcotics sachets than the naïve pups because the previous experience familiarized them with the narcotics odour. This would be considered social facilitation.

Alternatively, the observer pups saw both their dam and the trainer making a fuss over these sachets, so when they had the opportunity, these pups were more keen to investigate the sachets themselves. This is consistent with stimulus enhancement.

If you're still not convinced, then I have this question for you: if dogs are capable of learning by imitation, why would they not do it all the time? It is such an efficient form of learning that I fail to understand why dogs wouldn't use the capacity frequently. It sure would make training a lot easier!

The ability to learn by imitation requires that the observer is able to imagine himself as the demonstrator—to put himself in the other's shoes, so to speak. Very young children lack this capacity and they are also unable to imitate until they achieve this developmental milestone.

It is likely that most animal species—except the great apes—also lack this cognitive ability. Despite the efficiency of imitation, it appears to be an adaptation too costly to evolve in most creatures. So, in the end, there is a good reason why the saying is "monkey see, monkey do" rather than "doggy see, doggy do!"

2011 update

Since I wrote this piece, there have been a couple of studies on dogs' capacity for imitation. Both studies attempted a version of the two-action test. In one, dogs were taught to pull on a handle with either their mouth or their paw to release a piece of food. Dogs then watched a demonstration of one of the two actions. The researchers wanted to know if the observer dogs were biased toward the action they saw being performed by the demonstrator. The results were somewhat convincing, but the original conclusions have since been discredited by additional findings using the same apparatus.

A second study involved dogs watching a human or a dog demonstrator push a curtain aside to gain access to food. Some observer dogs saw the curtain being pushed to the left; others saw it pushed to the right. When the observer dogs were given the opportunity to move the curtain themselves, most pushed in same direction that they had seen in the demonstration. While this finding is fascinating, it's still consistent with an explanation of stimulus enhancement. Dogs saw the curtain move in one direction and, when they found themselves in the same situation, they grabbed the curtain and were drawn to move in that same direction. In fact, dogs were also likely to move the curtain in the same direction as they saw when the curtain moved on its own, with no human or dog demonstration. Thus, there is no need for the dog to have the capacity to reason that by copying what the demonstrator did, it will also receive food.

TEMPERAMENT
TESTING
Debated Validity, Valuable Information

The puppy buyer gazes at the German Shepherd puppies. They all seem to have their own distinct personalities: one is a bit timid; one is very cuddly and always licking everyone; one plays constantly; and one is a feisty little girl trying her best to herd all the others. Which one to choose? Is there a way to know which puppy will be the best companion?

What is temperament?
Temperament or 'personality' is a catch-all term for a number of elements, such as sociability, excitability, sensitivity, confidence, and playfulness. How is a dog's temperament determined? It's believed that a puppy is born with certain traits or predispositions and that, as the puppy develops, these traits are molded and refined by experience. Temperament is the result of the interaction between this 'raw material' and environmental influences.

Assessing the raw material
Is there some way for the buyer to ascertain the temperament of these puppies *before* they're influenced by experience? Gail Fisher and Wendy Volhard have developed a test called the Puppy Aptitude Test (PAT) which is intended to do exactly that. The puppy temperament test is administered when the litter is forty-nine days of age—roughly the age at which puppy brain activity, measured by

Electroencephalogram (EEG), first matches the pattern of an adult dog. Fisher and Volhard believe that behaviour at this age provides the best indication of temperament without environmental influences.

The PAT consists of a set of exercises designed to evaluate sociability and sensory capacities. First, the puppy's inclination to approach and follow a stranger in an unfamiliar environment is assessed. Then, the tester observes the puppy's willingness to accept being restrained on his back and in the air. The tester assigns a numerical score that reflects the puppy's friendliness and compliance. Next, the puppy is encouraged to play with and chase a ball of paper to determine his proclivity for retrieving. Finally, the puppy's awareness of his environment is evaluated by exposing him to tactile (a pinch on the webbing between the toes), auditory (a loud startling sound), and visual (a cloth dragged across the ground in front of the puppy) stimuli. Reactions to these experiences are intended to indicate the puppy's suitability for obedience training.

What do the results mean?

Do the results of the PAT predict anything about how the puppy will behave generally? In order for the PAT to be considered predictive of temperament, we need confirmation that the behaviours observed during the test are highly correlated with the puppy's behaviours in a variety of situations and, ideally, with adult behaviour.

Fisher and Volhard believe that the PAT is a predictive tool. They developed the test to reveal genetically based behavioural tendencies so breeders can identify which puppies will be most suitable for companionship and/or obedience training.

Three Canadian researchers measured the validity of the sociability components of the PAT. A small number of puppies were tested at seven weeks and again at sixteen weeks. They found very little correlation between how the puppies behaved across the two tests. The only clear result was that puppies dominant at seven weeks tended to be more neutral at sixteen weeks, and puppies neutral at seven weeks were more likely to be submissive at sixteen weeks. I suspect that this was not due to a change in temperament as much as it was related to the fact that puppies tend to be more inhibited in an unfamiliar situation once they are no longer in the midst of their socialization period (which typically ends around the sixteenth week).

Other temperament tests

Other tests of puppy temperament are designed for a specific purpose, such as selecting puppies for guide-dog training. In fact, guide-dog selection has been subjected to rigorous study. In Clarence Pfaffenberger's original work *The New Knowledge of Dog Behavior*, puppies were tested once a week from their eighth through twelfth weeks of age. Test items were simulations of real-life guiding experiences, such as navigating under a hanging ledge and avoiding a fast-moving cart. In later tests, puppies that did well on the test consistently outperformed puppies that did not. Surprisingly, two items—the puppy's inclination to retrieve and his reaction to a fast-moving cart moving directly toward him—turned out to be quite predictive of future success. Once puppies were selected on the basis of the test, the proportion of dogs that successfully completed guide-dog training went from eight percent to over ninety percent!

Temperament tests for adult dogs are usually designed to select a dog for a particular purpose, such as detection work, protection training or Schutzhund. The United States Border Patrol instituted an extensive training procedure for selecting dogs from shelters. Since the inception of this system, the failure rate in the detection training program has decreased dramatically.

The American Temperament Test Society has a battery of test items intended to provide a general picture of the adult dog's reaction to real-life experiences, such as unusual footing, an opening umbrella, and a menacing stranger. Some people like to take this test primarily to determine if their dog would protect them in a threatening situation. I was floored when my Saluki stood in front of me, barking and growling at the threatening person. A few months later, he did the same to a burglar who entered our home in the middle of the night.

Researchers in the Netherlands developed a test to help animal shelters identify which dogs are at risk for displaying behaviour problems in their new homes. The test consists of various experiences, including a friendly stranger approaching the cage, taking the dog for a walk, engaging the dog in play, having a life-sized doll on wheels approach the dog, removing the food bowl while the dog is eating, introducing him to an unfamiliar dog and leaving the dog alone in a car for ten minutes. They correlated their findings with opinions from the shelter staff and then followed up with the new owners to ascertain the nature of any problem behaviour. They reported an accurate prediction of problem behaviour in seventy-five percent of the eighty-one dogs tested.

Are temperament tests worthwhile?

Obviously, obtaining a personality profile of a puppy would be extremely useful for breeders and puppy buyers. We don't know the value of available temperament tests because their predictive validity has not been properly assessed. Even personality tests for people are fraught with similar questions of validity.

Emphasis needs to be placed on continuing research, which will eventually provide the answers. This work is extremely important because so many behaviour problems develop due to a mismatch between dog and owner. With the evaluation and refinement of temperament tests, we should one day be able to determine a great deal about our canine companions.

DOG BEHAVIOUR PROFESSIONALS

It Is Critical for Consumers to be Informed

You get the call most breeders dread: "Help, we can't keep the dog because he's growling at our new baby" or "He's destroying the house when we leave him alone." It might be a puppy from your last litter or a mature dog that you haven't seen in years. The owner is distraught and really doesn't want to give up the dog. You want to make sure there's a happy ending to the story for everyone.

One of your options is to suggest they seek advice from an expert in animal behaviour. But how do you select someone from the myriad of professionals proclaiming their expertise? There are dog trainers, certified pet dog trainers, canine behaviourists, behaviour counselors, aggression specialists, dog psychologists, veterinarians who advise on behaviour, applied animal behaviourists, clinical ethologists, and veterinary behaviourists. What do all these titles mean?

A buyer beware market

The field of clinical animal behaviour is not well regulated and most of these titles can be donned by anyone. Some professionals will possess impeccable academic qualifications, but little or no real life experience; others will have plenty of hands-on wisdom, but no formal education. Others will have both and some will have none. The better the credentials, the more secure you can be in assuming that the professional is competent, but there are no guarantees. The proof is in the pudding.

What does certification mean?

There are numerous certifying organizations for pet dog trainers, including the Certification Counsel for Pet Dog Trainers, the International Association of Canine Professionals and the International Association of Animal Behaviour Counselors. All vary in their requirements but look for proficiency in both training principles and practical experience. Steer clear of the schools that educate trainers and then turn around and certify their own graduates—an objective and unbiased certification program will be independent of the school that offers the education.

There are presently two internationally recognized organizations that certify academically-trained clinical animal behaviourists: The Animal Behaviour Society and The American College of Veterinary Behaviourists.

The Animal Behaviour Society (ABS) is the oldest certification program for people holding the advanced degrees of DVM, Master of Arts or Science, and Ph.D. The Board of Professional Certification recognizes two levels of competency: Certified Applied Animal Behaviourist (CAAB) (Ph.D. or DVM level) and Associate Certified Applied Animal Behaviourist (ACAAB) (MA or MSc level). Eligibility is open to those with Masters or Ph.D. degrees studied in an animal-behaviour related discipline, such as psychology, ethology or zoology. Individuals with a DVM will have completed a residency in behaviour under the supervision of a certified behaviourist. Applicants must present proof of academic credentials (including specific courses in learning theory, ethology, comparative psychology and research design), an account of clinical experience, detailed case studies, evidence of original contributions to the field (research, publications, etc.), and letters of recommendation.

CAABs and ACAABs are deemed academically, experientially and ethically qualified to treat behaviour problems in animals. They are required to abide by a strict code of ethics regarding their professional conduct and their treatment of animals. In fact, ABS-certified behaviourists must not guarantee their results because they recognize that behaviour is a complex phenomenon—no one can be certain of successfully resolving any type of behaviour problem. Every five years, CAABs and ACAABS must be re-certified.

Veterinary behaviourists are certified by the American College of Veterinary Behaviourists. In order to be qualified to sit for the exam, a veterinarian must have completed a two- to three-year residency under a veterinary behaviourist. The resident must submit credentials, case studies and letters of reference to a board that determines whether the person is qualified to sit. If the person is approved, they must pass an exam that consists of questions on ethology, psychology, pharmacology, neuroscience and internal medicine.

Guiding your choice

Should you send your distraught owner to a trainer, a veterinarian, a veterinary behaviourist or an applied animal behaviourist? This question has to be answered on an individual basis. Education doesn't mean a person is competent, but neither does experience. Certification means the person meets or exceeds certain standards but says nothing about the person's proficiency.

I can't claim to be unbiased in my opinion, but I believe that complex behaviour problems are more likely to be resolved by someone with a sound background in both theory and experience. Most behaviour problems result from a complicated interplay between the pet and its family so a flexible range of potential recommendations is most likely to be beneficial. Knowledge of theory and principles prepares the person to devise novel solutions when the situation demands them.

I would like to see trainers, veterinarians and behaviourists work together to provide assistance to people living with problem dogs. A useful analogy might be the system in place for children with developmental or behavioural problems. In the early stages, a parent would likely approach the child's teacher (analogous to the pet's trainer) and their pediatrician (the pet's veterinarian) for help. These people might refer to a specialist right away or they might offer sound advice that is generally helpful.

If this guidance doesn't help within a reasonable time period, the parent is advised to see a child psychologist (analogous to an applied animal behaviourist). If the child would benefit from medication, they are further referred to a psychiatrist (veterinary behaviourist). In some cases, the psychologist might counsel the child and parents directly, while for other cases, the psychologist advises the teacher on implementing helpful changes.

Likewise, the owner of a dog with a behaviour problem should first speak to the trainer and the veterinarian for preliminary advice. If this doesn't resolve the problem, the owner is referred to an applied animal behaviourist for a detailed examination of the situation. If medication is indicated, the counsel of a veterinary behaviourist should be sought. If you find yourself in an area that is not serviced by a qualified behaviourist, you can still request a referral to someone who counsels over the telephone or via email, although many will only accept aggression cases on an in-person basis because of safety and liability concerns.

Educational opportunities

I am frequently asked how someone enters the field of applied animal behaviour. Becoming a certified behaviourist takes years of postgraduate education and training, either at a university or veterinary college. Most good-sized universities will have at least one professor who researches animal behaviour, although it is unlikely to be with companion animals. You'll still learn the principles of behaviour, learning and research which you can apply to any species. For more information on graduate programs in animal behaviour, check the Animal Behavior Society web site at www.animalbehaviorsociety.org.

Can the dog be helped?

That's impossible to answer without knowing details about the dog, the family and the problem. Typically, behaviour problems are so complex that simple advice like "take obedience classes" or "stop spoiling the dog" are probably not going to suffice. In fact, one study found dogs that had received obedience training were no less likely to develop behaviour problems than dogs with little or no training.

Furthermore, when owners were queried about how much they spoiled their dogs, there was no match with behaviour problems and the tendency to spoil. Behaviour is rarely straightforward!

Can a behaviour specialist help? Sometimes—but not always. A competent, ethical behaviourist will be able to provide a reasonable guess as to the dog's prognosis, based on his or her clinical experience and knowledge of the literature. If appropriate, the behaviourist can discuss other options, such as rehoming and euthanasia. Owners are often more comfortable arriving at such a decision if they have received guidance from a behaviour professional and feel they have done everything reasonable to resolve the problem. The ultimate goal of a behaviourist should be to achieve, in a safe and humane manner, a harmonious relationship between the dog and owner.

As with any unregulated profession, it is critical for consumers to be informed. When advising puppy owners on seeking help for behaviour problems, check the behaviourist's qualifications and references. Ask plenty of questions. Make sure you understand and are completely comfortable with the recommended suggestions. The more you know, the more likely you will succeed!

Part Two

TRAINING

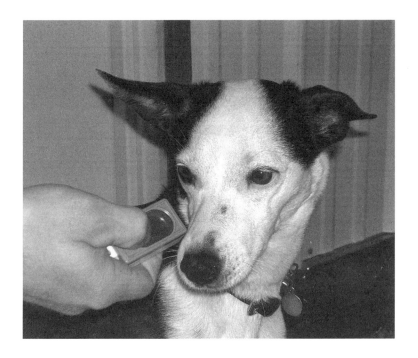

There's nothing quite as intimate as mentoring a young puppy as he learns something about the world. Everything is so fresh and new. It's as though you've been given the opportunity to glimpse, albeit indirectly, into the workings of the little guy's mind. It saddens me that so many dogs and their guardians never share the type of relationship that fosters mutual discovery and communication. Teaching gets us as close to a cross-species conversation as we will ever realize.

I'll never forget the excitement I felt when I took my first undergraduate university course in learning theory. Sure, the textbook was dense and the professor was dry at times but right away, I recognized the potential applications. If I could master what we know about how animals learn in a laboratory, I could find out how well it all maps onto training in the real world. I had my work cut out for me because at the time, I was the proud guardian of a baby Saluki and I was determined that he would be my first competitive obedience dog. I'd already heard that Salukis were independent, cat-like and, above all, stupid. Those descriptions just weren't sitting well with what I was experiencing. Shaahiin was inquisitive, interactive and insightful. He made connections between things quite readily. He seemed to me to be quite clever. I soon learned that there's a major distinction between intelligence and trainability! And I came to admire the person who said "In theory there is no difference between theory and practice. In practice, there is."[1] Shaahiin challenged what I was learning in the classroom at every opportunity. And he inspired me to become an innovative and determined trainer. We went on to put in some very respectable performances in the obedience ring and he became a breed pioneer in the sports of flyball and agility—sports that were just emerging at the time.

In this section, I introduce the reader to some of the basic tenets of learning theory: operant and respondent conditioning; clicker training; motivation; the effects of context; and the ethics of using 'corrections.' Obviously, there are complexities and nuances to learning theory that could, and do, fill the pages of countless books. For the academically inclined, here are a few of my favourites:

---

[1]This quote has been attributed to numerous people, most often to Jan L. A. van de Snepscheut and Yogi Berra.

- Mark Bouton's *Learning and Behavior: A Contemporary Synthesis*
- Sara Shettlworth's *Cognition, Evolution, and Behavior.*
- Michael Domjan's *The Principles of Learning and Behavior*
- N.J. Mackintosh's *The Psychology of Animal Learning.*

OPERANT
CONDITIONING
A New Magical Training Tool?

I hear some dog trainers claim that they are purely positive in their methods because they use operant conditioning. For instance, in the August 2000 *AKC Gazette*, Karen Pryor referred to operant conditioning as "the art of training behaviour without using force or punishment." Unfortunately this creates confusion because operant conditioning includes any learning in which the dog's behaviour is instrumental in producing a consequence. The dog might do something which produces a pleasant consequence or an unpleasant consequence—both are examples of operant conditioning.

The ABC's of operant conditioning
Operant conditioning follows a specific sequence: Antecedent → Behaviour → Consequence.

The antecedent is the cue or command used to signal the dog to perform a behaviour. It could also be any situation that triggers a specific behaviour to occur. The behaviour is what the dog does and this behaviour leads to a consequence. Whether the dog continues to perform the behaviour is a result of the consequence. Thorndike's Law of Effect describes how this works: if a consequence is pleasant, the preceding behaviour becomes more likely; if a consequence is unpleasant, the preceding behaviour becomes less likely.

The power of consequences

There are four ways that influential consequences can occur. For instance, a guest comes to the door and your dog jumps up. The guest makes a fuss over the dog and the dog enjoys it. This is **positive reinforcement** because the guest presented something pleasant (attention) and the dog is more likely to jump up the next time a guest arrives. The term "reinforcement" refers to the fact that the preceding behaviour becomes more likely. The term "positive" signifies that the guest added something. *It does not symbolize that the dog likes it.*

Alternatively, the guest could have presented the dog with something unpleasant by kneeing the dog in the chest when he jumped up. (I am not recommending this because it could injure or frighten the dog.) This is **positive punishment** if the dog is less likely to jump up on guests again. "Punishment" refers to the fact that the preceding behaviour becomes less likely. It is positive because the guest is still adding something—in this case, something aversive to the dog.

Instead of the consequence involving the presentation of something pleasant or unpleasant, the consequence could be the *removal* of something pleasant or unpleasant. Suppose the dog jumps up on the guest and the guest turns away and faces the wall until the dog stops jumping. This would be **negative punishment** if the dog is less likely to jump up on guests again. Why? Because jumping up led to the *removal* of something pleasant. The dog wanted the guest's attention but, when he jumped up, the guest ignored him. It is still punishment because the preceding behaviour becomes less likely. The term "negative" signifies that the guest removed something. *It does not symbolize that the dog doesn't like it.*

In the final scenario, the dog sits nicely at the door and the guest reaches down to shake the dog's paw. The guest shakes the dog's paw so roughly that the dog jumps up at the person. The person lets go of the dog's paw. This is **negative reinforcement** if the dog found the rough shaking unpleasant and discovered that the behaviour of jumping up stopped the unpleasantness. It is reinforcement because the jumping-up behaviour is more likely to happen the next time someone touches the dog's paw. It is negative because the guest removed something. One of the easiest ways to conceive of negative reinforcement is to think of it as escape or avoidance. The dog was able to escape rough handling by jumping up at the person.

Real life examples

Much of our dogs' behaviour and our own behaviour is governed by operant conditioning. You will quickly realize, however, that these consequences rarely occur in isolation. Rewards are given (positive reinforcement) or withheld (negative punishment), depending upon behaviour. Behaviour that leads to something unpleasant is inhibited (positive punishment), while a different behaviour is often expressed in order to avoid the unpleasantness again (negative reinforcement). Examples of behaviours maintained primarily through positive reinforcement abound. We work hard on a project at work to earn the approval of our peers. Our dogs bark at the cookie jar because we are likely to give them a treat.

Much behaviour is governed by positive punishment. As children, we learned to inhibit swearing in front of our parents because it results in scolding. Our dogs refrain from urinating in the house or chewing the furniture because these behaviours cause us to reprimand them. One dog learns to stay out of another dog's bed because once it led to a fight.

Examples of behaviours governed by negative punishment are also prevalent. As children, we learned not to have a temper tantrum or we would have to go to our rooms. Our dogs learn not to behave too rambunctiously or they are banished to the back yard.

Finally, there is behaviour maintained through negative reinforcement. We wear seatbelts to avoid the nasty buzzing sound in the car and to avoid being badly injured in an accident. Our dogs learn to play catch-me-if-you-can to avoid coming home from the park. Dogs that live with electronic containment systems stay inside the property boundary to avoid being shocked.

The bottom line

Operant conditioning is not a new discovery nor is it some type of magical training tool. It is a term that describes any behaviour that is controlled by its consequences. Reward-based training emphasizes specific components of operant conditioning: positive reinforcement and negative punishment. Compulsive training incorporates some degree of negative reinforcement and positive punishment. Both training philosophies are based on operant conditioning methods.

Pushing the Right Button

The Secret to Changing Your Dog's Emotional Response

Does your dog drool when he hears the timer rings on the microwave? My dogs do because I often microwave veggies to add to their meals. The first research on drooling dogs was done by Ivan Pavlov, a Nobel-prize-winning physiologist and a founding father of the science of how animals learn. He studied the salivary reflex by measuring the amount of drool produced by hungry dogs while they ate tasty food. Pavlov discovered that, after a bit of experience, dogs started salivating as soon as they were brought into the room where the research was being conducted. Fascinated by the dogs' anticipation, Pavlov wondered if he had discovered an important clue to understanding the learning processes of animals. He tested his idea formally by ringing a bell just before presenting food and, sure enough, the dogs began salivating to the bell. Pavlov called this ability to connect different events "associative learning."

Pavlov's learning by association ("what goes with what") underlies much of how our dogs acquire emotional responses. A puppy quickly learns that a particular sound (which we humans recognize as his name) comes to be associated with a variety of good experiences, such as treats, play, walks and cuddles.

Associative learning can produce negative emotions too. The sight of nail clippers causes many dogs to run and hide because, in the past, clippers have been associated with trauma to their toes. The smell of a veterinary clinic causes my Saluki to have a full-blown panic attack because years ago he learned to associate that smell with a painful injury and the resulting treatments.

Unintended learning

Consider the adolescent dog whose owner, during obedience class, constantly pulls him away from greeting other dogs and people. What is he learning? Imagine how you'd feel if every time you approached a person to say hello, your guardian angel slapped you on the arm and scolded you for your behaviour. I suspect you'd become pretty apprehensive around people.

Most dogs don't learn to refrain from sniffing dogs and jumping on people just by being pulled away repeatedly. Instead, they learn that a dog or a person nearby usually predicts an uncomfortable yank on the neck, and, in some cases, this leads to a dog that still appears to want to say hello but then behaves fearfully or aggressively when he gets up close.

Undoing an association

Molly, a young Puli, is uncomfortable around people she doesn't know. Molly's previous owners always crated her when guests came, and visiting children teased her through the bars. She soon learned to fear and loathe people. For many fearful dogs, the best defense is a good offense and Molly is no exception: her way of dealing with her fear is to bark, growl and bite.

Changing Molly's behaviour requires that she learn a new association: this is called counter-conditioning because the original association is replaced with a new association that is counter to the original. The tricky part is that the original association is not erased—in order for counter-conditioning to work, the new positive association must, on balance, out-weigh the old negative association. For example, Molly's new owners decided to have visitors bring lots of goodies to her. This can work, but only if Molly's desire for the goodies is stronger than her fear of being near strangers.

Some dogs solve the dilemma by first eating the goodies and then biting the guest! The treats draw the dog too close for comfort and, once the treats are gone, fear overwhelms the dog. I prefer to have visitors toss the food—that way the dog can maintain a comfortable distance from the stranger. The guest should continue tossing food until the dog is relaxed and comfortable. Then it is relatively safe to offer the treats and, finally, to scratch the dog under the chin. This may take a few minutes for some dogs, several months for others.

Another complication of counter-conditioning is that it will work only if the bad thing consistently and reliably predicts the good thing. In Molly's case, she needs to learn that visitors signal the arrival of goodies. This means Molly should not have the goodies when visitors are not present. I discovered this first hand when I tried to counter-condition my response to house cleaning. I *hate* cleaning, so my husband suggested I counter-condition myself to like it by eating my favorite food (chocolate) while cleaning.

This might sound like a great idea, but it didn't work because I also ate chocolate when I wasn't cleaning the house. It would be very different, however, if I, or someone else, restricted my access to chocolate so that I only had access to it while cleaning. Once I could *only* eat chocolate while cleaning the house, I enjoyed cleaning more.

Molly had a passion for boiled chicken livers so her owners always had some on hand in case visitors dropped by. They skipped Molly's meal on days they expected company so she'd be especially hungry. A note next to a container of liver outside the door provided instructions to the visitors. When the doorbell rang, Molly was required to sit in a spot where she could see the goings-on at the front door, but she couldn't reach the people. The guests tossed her liver from the doorway. They tossed her liver as they walked into the living room. They tossed liver all over the floor around them before sitting. They covered their feet and legs with liver! Molly was then released from her spot to greet the guests. She was kept on a head halter and leash just in case things didn't go as planned. Of course she paid little attention to the guests—she was too busy feeding from the floor. That was just fine.

When she finally did get to the visitors, they functioned like food dishes. While Molly gobbled up the food, the guests sat very still and did not look at or speak to her. Any growling or barking was ignored. Once the liver was gone, Molly's owner gave her a stuffed Kong. Still on-leash, she lay down next to her owner and worked at the Kong for the remainder of the visit.

As soon as the guests prepared to leave, more liver was tossed to keep Molly focused on the floor rather than on the people. Once the guests were gone, the liver and the Kong likewise disappeared. After many visits, Molly began to drool like Pavlov's dogs whenever the doorbell rang. Because she was hungry and her owners used a highly desirable food, the good things she came to associate with visitors were strong enough to overcome the negative association she had learned previously.

Rewarding bad behaviour?

Would it matter if Molly still barked and growled while the guests tossed treats to her? It may be hard to believe but it wouldn't. Because the barking and growling are manifestations of an underlying negative emotion, if you change the emotion, you change the symptoms too. As soon as Molly stopped hating strangers, she didn't feel the need to bark and growl anymore. That's the immense clout of counter-conditioning!

Pavlov stumbled onto a powerfully effective way to teach animals. Counter-conditioning can be used to change any type of emotional response, from a dog that fears the vacuum cleaner to a dog that resents being moved from the bed. The underlying logic is simple: if the bad event predicts a good event, the bad will become good. The only catch is that the good thing must be 'more good' to the dog than the bad thing is bad!

WILL WORK FOR FOOD

Finding the Key that Drives Your Dog

Competing with a Saluki in obedience and other performance sports taught me a great deal about creativity in training. Despite Stanley Coren's assertion in his book, *The Intelligence of Dogs,* that Sighthounds rate low on the intelligence scale, my experience suggests these breeds are quick to learn but extraordinarily difficult to motivate. Motivation is what drives an animal to engage in certain behaviours. Motivation is just as crucial as learning when it comes to training dogs. Learning is the how, motivation is the why in training.

Dogs perform the behaviours we teach them because they're motivated to do so. That motivation exists because we offer the dog something he wants or something he prefers to avoid. Following are motivational techniques that emphasize food, play, and other activities dogs enjoy.

Driving the dog

Some trainers view motivation in terms of what 'drives' the dog. They talk of dogs with prey drive, social drive, play drive and so on. As a scientific construct, drive theory was popular several decades ago, but it fell from favour when psychologists realized that proposing a lengthy list of drives didn't really explain an animal's behaviour. Instead, psychologists turned their attentions toward understanding what factors influence motivation. The present notion of drives gives us a way to describe those dogs that are highly motivated to engage in certain behaviours, such as chasing or swimming, or those dogs that seem to regard training itself as highly reinforcing.

"Will work for food"

Depriving a dog of things that he needs or wants increases motivation. A hungry dog will work for food whereas a dog that has just eaten a meal will be less interested in training. I rarely fed my Saluki, Shaahiin, the night before a competition so he'd be especially enthusiastic about the food rewards I offered. Likewise, a dog that has just been out for a ten mile run will not be so thrilled with a game of tug as a dog that has slept most of the day.

Be aware that you can overdo deprivation: excessive food, exercise or attention deprivation actually disrupts learning. Beyond a certain level of deprivation, more is not better.

Deprivation has its greatest effect when the dog is learning something new. Imagine that you are teaching your dog to come when called. A hungry dog will run faster than a satiated dog. Once the dog has learned the exercise, even if the dog is no longer hungry, he will continue to run faster because he learned to perform the response quickly. When my dog Eej was a pup, I deprived him of tennis balls except during flyball training. I kept all the balls in a drawer and I'd occasionally open the drawer and show him a ball, but I wouldn't let him touch it. By the time flyball practice came around each Tuesday, he was itching to get his mouth on a ball. Now, even though balls are scattered about the house, they are still one of Eej's favourite toys.

What's in a reward?

The standard fare for a dog's job well done is a small tidbit or a bout of play with a preferred toy. Most dogs are quite happy with this. If offered a choice, however, the average dog has clear preferences for certain types of treats or certain types of play over others. Soft, smelly foods are generally favoured by food-motivated dogs. Shaahiin's favorite food was pizza and I was able to get him to run almost half a second faster in flyball when I had a slice of pizza stashed in the ball bucket! For play, I find interactive games like tug and tag to be fun for the dog and best for forming a close working relationship with the trainer.

Animals also have a concept of number, and in this department, more is definitely better. Dogs enjoy the act of eating, so they get more pleasure from eating numerous small treats than one large treat. This explains the popularity of food toys, like the Kong and the Buster Cube, which draws out the eating experience. As a rule, the higher the value of the reward, whether it is tastier or greater in number, the more enthusiastically the dog will work for it.

Rewards need not be restricted to food and play. Anything that the dog enjoys can be used to reinforce good behaviour, provided you can control the dog's access to it. I've used car rides, play with a water hose, kicking leaves, and the chance to chase a squirrel or attack the blow dryer as motivators in training. Once, while laying a track, I found a dead groundhog—a high value reward for a Saluki! I placed it at the end of the track and Shaahiin's reward was rolling on a smelly corpse!

The dog's expectation of what he's going to receive as a reward also impacts his motivation. When Shaahiin and I were training, I used wieners as the usual reward but, prior to going into the ring to compete, I'd let him sniff and maybe even taste something far more tantalizing, like leftover roast beef, salami or an odorous liver muffin. His performances were usually more invigorated, a result known as the 'elation effect.' I called this technique giving the dog a 'jumpstart!'

Related is the trick of giving a dog a 'jackpot' of a super-duper reward for an exceptional performance. I've heard claims that giving jackpots serves to enhance learning and that the jackpot 'stamps in' a memory for what the dog did to earn it. Research indicates that jackpots do little to influence learning per se—their effect is essentially the same as a jumpstart. A jackpot serves to charge up future performance but does little to communicate to the animal that his previous actions were special.

Firing the dog up

Building anticipation is a great way to get your dog to fire off the starting block. Dogs and people are alike in that they get excited as suspense mounts. Imagine what sprinters feel as they hear, "On your mark...get set...." and then the starter's pistol. You can get the same effect with your dog if you teach him that he gets to do really fun things on the "Go" or on the count of three. Eej conveys his intensity by barking when I count "One," then his body gets tense and his mouth starts to close on "Two," and by "Three," his body is a coiled spring, his mouth is closed tight, and he looks ready to spontaneously combust!

Adding fuel to the fire

Years ago a researcher taught hungry mice to run in a straight alleyway for food. The mice regularly found a piece of cheese halfway along the alley and another piece at the end. After many repetitions, the researcher neglected to put the cheese in the middle and to his surprise, he observed that the mice ran the last half of the alley faster than normal. The explanation? Not getting an expected reward leads to frustration and frustration energizes behaviour.

Frustration is the basis for why intermittent schedules of reinforcement result in a more intense response. The initial reaction of a frustrated animal is to try harder. Typically, the animal performs whatever behaviour has been successful in the past. If that fails, the frustration fuels the dog to try a new behaviour. In the case of intermittent reinforcement, the animal learns to continue trying, even in the face of non-reward, because trying eventually pays off.

The energy produced by frustration can be channeled into the behaviour you want by combining anticipation and temporary restraint. One of the first games I teach a puppy is the restrained recall. A friend holds the puppy by the collar or chest while I tease the puppy with a favourite toy or treat. I take off running as fast as I can go and the friend eggs the puppy on, encouraging him to struggle to get away and pursue me. After a few seconds of struggling, the puppy is released to chase me and earn his reward. This teaches the puppy that the frustration associated with restraint should be directed into continued struggling and faster running. Dogs that know this game usually accelerate hard on recalls.

Lighting a spark

A minority of dogs remain uninspired despite a trainer's best efforts at motivation. You try to spark the fire but it's as though the pilot light is out. Dogs fail to work at their best for a variety of reasons, ranging from incomplete learning to performance anxiety. The key to solving a motivation problem is identifying the source of the problem. Dogs that shut down from stress are the most challenging because the trainer needs to take measures to reduce stress and build confidence. At the same time, the dog needs to learn to focus and work despite the stress.

The super-charged dog

Learning and motivation are interlinked components of the training game. Teaching a dog something new is relatively easy; motivating him to perform can be a lot more challenging. In many cases, an apparently 'dumb' dog may learn quickly but have little reason to perform the learned behaviour. Shaahiin rarely required more than a few repetitions to learn something new but I was constantly forced to stay one step ahead of him, seeking new ways to fuel his fire. A skilled trainer uses games to strengthen the dog's drive and capitalizes on anticipation and frustration to fire the dog up to super-charged triumphs.

TRAINING DOGS, CLICKETY-SPLIT

The Clicker Has Taken the Dog World by Storm

Wanna know what's hip and trendy in the dog world? In-the-know dogs these days are grooving to a new sound. They no longer get excited by, "Good dog" or "Atta boy"—it's now 'click.' Dog enthusiasts and trainers have taken to clicker training like ducks to water. I hear clicking at agility trials, obedience competitions, flyball tournaments, even at the local city park. What is this craze?

Clicker training is extremely simple. It is reward-based training with the use of a sound—the click—that the dog learns to associate with the delivery of reinforcement. The dog learns that when he hears a click, a reward is on its way.

Why would you want to incorporate this extra step? Because dogs repeat behaviours that have good consequences for them. The click, which comes *after* the behaviour but *before* the treat, makes it very clear to the dog exactly which behaviour produced the treat. It helps to think of the click as though you are taking a snapshot of the behaviour you are teaching the dog—you click at exactly the moment the dog performs the behaviour. The clicker is often called a "marker" because it precisely identifies the desired behaviour.

For example, suppose you are teaching your dog to lie down. There are a variety of ways to get your dog to lie down, the simplest of which involve the dog moving from a Sit into the Down. If the dog's butt is already sitting, then a Down can be defined as when the dog's elbows hit the floor. An astute clicker trainer times the click so that it sounds at precisely the moment the dog's elbows make contact with the floor, to mark this exact behaviour. The dog comes to learn that the way to earn a treat is to get those elbows on the ground fast.

What's in a click?

Is there something magical about the click sound? Not at all. In fact, you could use anything at all—a flashing light, a touch, a special word—provided that it reliably signals the reward. However, sounds are more practical because the dog doesn't have to be next to you nor does it have to be looking at you to perceive a sound. Words can be substituted for the click—I prefer to use the word "Yes" than to fumble around with a clicker in my hand while I'm running around an agility course. However, the clicker has a distinct advantage over a word in that it always sounds exactly the same, whereas I might be tempted to say "Yes" with different intonations depending upon how pleased I am with my dog's performance. And the click is a relatively unique sound—unless you speak the language of the Kalahari, your dog doesn't hear clicks in your general conversations. I say "Yes" on a frequent basis and my dog has learned to tell the difference between "Yes" when I'm communicating with him and when I'm talking with people.

Training with a clicker has its roots firmly embedded in the laboratory of the famous experimental psychologist B.F. Skinner, the father of operant conditioning. He developed what came to be called a Skinner Box—a small box made for a rat, with a lever on one wall and a feeder situated just below. Skinner taught a hungry rat to press the bar with its paw, by rewarding it with food. He noticed that the rat needed to learn the association between the sound of the feeder mechanism and food dropping into container. A quiet feeder hampered the rat's progress because it was not clear to the animal what behaviour caused the food to appear. Skinner called the sound that becomes linked to the delivery of food a *conditioned reinforcer* because it comes to function a lot like the food itself. The clicker, because it is linked with food, functions as a conditioned reinforcer for dogs.

Dr. Skinner explained how a conditioned reinforcer could be used to train animals in the real world. He wrote a paper in which he described how you might teach a dog to open the cupboard door, using a conditioned reinforcer. First, you wait until the dog looks in the direction of the cupboard. You immediately make a distinctive noise—Skinner recommended a little device called a cricket that used to be sold as a child's toy—and then give the dog a treat. Eventually, the dog will look at the cupboard again, an action that produces another click and a treat. With plenty of patience and good timing, the dog will progressively learn to move toward the cupboard and nudge the door open, all through the judicious use of a clicking sound and treats.

Marine mammal trainers embraced Skinner's methods and developed an impressive program of reward-based training for their animals. They used whistles, rather than a clicker, to signal fish rewards, because the whistle sound travels through water more effectively. Dolphins and killer whales learned complex jumping and diving routines, sea lions learned to stand up and clap, and seals learned to walk on their flippers.

The conditioned reinforcer was especially important in this context because the animals had to return to the trainers for their rewards. The whistle served as a 'bridge' to span the time between performing the behaviour and being awarded the fish. As long as the whistle follows immediately after the behaviour, the animal still associates the reward with the behaviour it performed. In fact, many trainers call the clicker a bridge for this reason.

Charging the clicker

When Skinner worked with a rat, the first thing he did was teach the rat the significance of the feeder sound. Likewise, I always recommend teaching the dog to associate the click with treats prior to using the clicker for training behaviours. This is called *loading* or *charging* the clicker.

I sit with the dog and, at random points in time, click and give the dog a treat. It doesn't take him long to learn to orient to me instantly when he hears the click sound, in anticipation of a treat. I liken this process to charging a battery. The clicker now has acquired a certain amount of 'charge' for training. Each time the click is followed by a treat, it accrues a bit more charge. If the dog hears the click but doesn't get a treat, a bit of the charge drains from the clicker.

Some trainers advocate *never* clicking without giving a treat. I disagree—there is no harm at all in occasionally clicking without treating, provided that you 'recharge' it frequently. Once it is charged, the clicker has reinforcing properties all of its own and so you can reward behaviour without always giving your dog treats. You can train longer without your dog becoming full.

Must the clicker always be associated with food rewards? Some trainers prefer the clicker to signify a specific reward while others like to use a *generalized* conditioned reinforcer. This means that the clicker has been linked to a variety of rewards, such as treats, walks, play and cuddles.

The benefit of a generalized clicker is that it has power even when the dog is not hungry. However, the potency of your clicker might suffer because the sound does not elicit a specific motivation, such as feeding. Instead, the dog feels a general sense of pleasure, without knowing for certain what type of reward is in the offing.

Better training through science

Why has clicker training so revolutionized dog training? Training is essentially a problem-solving task for the dog—the dog has to figure out which of its behaviours have pleasant consequences so it can repeat them, and which have unpleasant consequences so it can repress them. Any procedure that assists the dog in solving training problems, by making the solutions easy to figure out, will accelerate the learning process and make dogs and trainers happy.

Clicker training, when used properly, can make learning quicker for dogs than training by more traditional methods. I recently decided to teach my clicker-savvy dog to rub his back on the ground on command. I waited until he rolled around to scratch his back. I clicked and gave him a treat. After only two clicks, he knew exactly which behaviour to perform and 'offered' it whenever I looked at him!

It's important to realize, however, that the clicker is merely a tool, derived from scientific research on behaviour. A tool is only as good as the person using it. If you are using the clicker to its fullest potential, your dog should prick up his ears whenever he hears the clicking sound and look to you for his reward. If your dog's reaction is anything less, you have either not charged the clicker correctly, you are using rewards that are not particularly motivating, or your training methods have confused your dog. A clicker in your hand is not a guarantee that your dog will learn more efficiently, but if you are using the tool properly, your dog will let you know by learning *clickety*-split!

Canine Stage Fright

Training for Reliable Performances

At a recent terrier fun day, I watched a young girl and her Jack Russell Terrier have a go in the trick competition. I was rooting for them because I had seen the girl earlier, next to her tent, practicing with the dog. They had an impressive routine. The dog did the usual beg, shake a paw and roll over but he also said his prayers, did a back flip and yawned on cue. I figured she'd be a shoe-in for first prize. I was taken by surprise, though, when it was their turn to perform for the judges. The dog, with his eyes glazed over, sniffed the ground as the anguished girl pleaded with him to perform. The more her voice conveyed her frustration, the less responsive the dog became, until the judges finally thanked her for her participation. The red ribbon and jar of cookies was awarded to a Cairn Terrier that barked along with her owner singing Happy Birthday.

Why had the JRT shut down? I had seen the dog performing accurately and happily only a few moments before. Dogs do seem to be prone to stage fright, but I doubt it's because they are worried or embarrassed about their ability to wow the crowds. Do dogs, like people, list fear of public performances as their number one dread, rated even higher than death? I suspect the answer, for dogs, is a lot simpler—the JRT wasn't prepared to generalize his training to this new situation.

Dolphin-trainer tales

At an Association of Pet Dog Trainers conference, I had the pleasure of attending a talk by behaviourist, Kathy Sdao. Sdao told us about the work she did training dolphins for the United States military. Her task was to teach wild-caught dolphins to perform search-and-rescue operations in the open ocean. She faced a number of interesting challenges. First, the dolphins had been removed from the wild only a few weeks earlier and Sdao's objective was to teach them to perform in the same ocean they'd been captured from, without confinement or restriction. How did she keep the dolphins from just swimming away? Second, she used strictly reward-based training and the reward she offered the dolphins was mackerel—dead mackerel—while the dolphins were swimming freely through schools of *live* mackerel. Sdao suggested this was much the same as training your dog while pork chops paraded around the room! Why didn't the dolphins just reward themselves? Third, in addition to mackerel, there were wild dolphins in the area and dolphins are extremely social creatures. Some of these animals were probably even friends and family of the trainees. You might expect that the dolphins would prefer to join up with their buddies than work for Sdao. And the last challenge? After a training session, the dolphins had to voluntarily jump onto the deck of the boat so they could be transported back to captivity in their small pens. What dolphin in its right mind would go along with this unlikely plan?

One small step at a time

How was Sdao able to succeed at such a difficult assignment? The answer lies in a sound knowledge of how to facilitate learning and performance. She started by teaching the rudimentary exercises in the dolphin's pen. There, a dead mackerel was an awesome treat. The dolphin could perform reliably and accurately because the small pen lacked the distractions that he would eventually face in open water. And the other plus? Jumping out of the pool onto the deck was a special opportunity to socialize with the trainer.

Sdao recognized the need for patient, systematic generalization training. Once the dolphin mastered the exercises in its home pen, the next step was to open two adjacent pens and put the dolphin through its paces in a slightly larger area. Sometimes another dolphin was present. From there, the dolphin was moved to gradually larger pens, occasionally with other animals. Small numbers of hard-to-catch fish were also introduced into the enclosures. The dolphins had the opportunity to learn that either they could catch their own meal or they could take the easy route and cajole Sdao into feeding them.

Sdao had each dolphin practice the behaviour of jumping into the boat a zillion times, with a quick release back into the water. Only once out of maybe every 50 times did jumping into the boat signal a return to the home pen. The penultimate baby step was to construct large pens in the ocean, where the dolphins would eventually be required to perform 'off the leash,' so to speak. These pens were moved around the bay to expose the dolphins to a variety of distractions, including wild dolphins. After all this, the transition to open water was no big deal for the dolphins. The impossible became achievable.

Resisting the urge to cut corners

We've all heard the owner who whines that his dog does the recall reliably in class but doesn't give him the time of day in the park. Or the owner who laments that his dog runs off as soon as he pulls out the leash to go home. Pet owners often fail to realize that dogs don't easily generalize training to new contexts, and that the park presents a myriad of wonderful distractions that can't compete with the standard fare of rewards we offer. Most professional trainers, on the other hand, know the importance of taking small incremental steps during training, but do we go to the lengths that Sdao did to ensure our dogs or our clients' dogs succeed? I suspect many of us, present company included, try to cut corners during the learning process, hoping the dogs will do well enough.

Sdao's talk served as a wake-up call for me. If you plan and implement your program intelligently and systematically, I suspect that you can train a dog to do just about anything, anywhere. Train many, many repetitions of each behaviour. Transition from the training context to the performance context in tiny gradations. Introduce minute distractions and gradually increase the complexity of the situation.

Work to ensure that your dog considers every opportunity to interact with you as the best fun ever. Challenge the dog, but don't ask for more than he's prepared to give.

A sure bet for the trickster

The tricky JRT was ready to perform backstage but he wasn't schooled for the limelight. He and his young accomplice would do well to go through their act numerous times—in front of friends, then receptive strangers, and finally, hecklers and critical judges. Once they're polished and toughened up, they'll be ready for awards night.

Saying "No"

How to Tell Your Dog He's Done Something Wrong

If you share your life with a dog, you are in the business of educating that dog. Teaching a dog involves two components: 1) encouraging behaviours you like; and 2) discouraging behaviours you dislike. Whether you are teaching your dog to be a top class competitor in your chosen sport or to be a well behaved member of your family, at some point your dog will do something you would prefer he not do again. Maybe he has chewed your favourite pair of shoes or urinated on the dining room rug. If he's an obedience dog, maybe he failed to bring you the dumbbell; if he's an agility dog, maybe he took a jump despite a clear signal from you to perform the tunnel; or, if he's a conformation dog, maybe he sat after you agonized over the perfect stack! How do you best convey to your dog when he has done something less than admirable?

Learning principles

Psychologists define punishment as any procedure that reduces the likelihood of a behaviour happening again. We think of punishment as involving something unpleasant for the dog, whether it be a harsh voice, a spank on the bum, a loud noise from a shake can or a spray of water in the face. These are examples of positive punishment—adding something aversive to stop the unwanted behaviour. However, there are procedures which fall under the term negative punishment—removing something the dog wants, to discourage unwanted behaviour.

Negative punishment procedures

There are various methods available to dog trainers that are based on the concept of negative punishment. The key to effective negative punishment is that the dog must expect to be rewarded but, instead, finds that the reward is not forthcoming. The conformation dog wants that bit of liver and tries sitting as a way to earn it. Upon sitting, the dog discovers that you put the bait back in your pouch. He then learns to try something different!

Parents use this procedure often to discourage undesirable behaviour in their children. The child refuses to eat his carrots at dinner—the parents withhold dessert until the carrots are gone. What about the child who shouts out in class? The teacher removes the child to the corner of the room where she sits while everyone else plays a fun game. Both children and dogs learn from negative punishment.

Extinction

Probably the most familiar negative punishment procedure is called *extinction*. Extinction makes good sense if you have inadvertently rewarded your dog for engaging in a behaviour that you later decide you don't like. Suppose your dog paws you while you're reading the paper and you absent-mindedly reach out and pet him. The next time he wants to be stroked, he's more likely to paw at you. If you continue to reward him, he will, in short order, reliably paw at you for attention and may even try pawing at you for other things he wants. If you now resolve to eliminate the behaviour by ignoring the dog whenever he paws at you, you are using an extinction procedure. The dog expects to be rewarded for the behaviour but, instead, gets no reaction. Once he learns this new arrangement, he will cease pawing because it no longer works.

Extinction is a powerful technique but it does have limitations. The unwanted behaviour can persist for quite a time, especially if it is a well established habit. In fact, the dog will actually paw at you more than normal at first because the behaviour has worked to this point. This is the same thing that happens when your car doesn't start—you don't give up right away. You keep trying and trying until, eventually, you call for help. Your dog goes through the same process.

Extinction works only if you can control the reward. You can't use extinction if the dog is chewing your favourite shoes because the reward for the dog is the feel and taste of the shoes. You can't use extinction to discourage your dog from sniffing on the agility course because you can't remove the pleasure he experiences from inhaling all those wonderful smells.

Counter-condition incompatible behaviour

One technique that enhances the effectiveness of extinction is counter-conditioning an incompatible behaviour. The idea is that if the dog is pawing you for attention, cease rewarding that behaviour but, at the same time, establish a behaviour that you do find acceptable to earn your attention. The dog still needs a method for communicating with you so it's best to design this method yourself rather than waiting for the dog to volunteer a new behaviour, which might be equally bad or worse than the current unacceptable behaviour. If you stick to extinction to get rid of the pawing behaviour, you might be successful, but very likely the dog will try barking, nudging with his nose or even leaping into your lap! Be proactive and teach him to sit and stare intently at you or vocalize quietly with *all four feet touching the floor*. The new behaviour is physically incompatible with the former behaviour of pawing and, even better, it gets your attention every single time. The technique is called counter-conditioning because you are conditioning a new behaviour that is *counter* to the originally conditioned behaviour. The original behaviour disappears because of extinction and because it is out-competed by the new behaviour.

Time out

Everyone has experienced a 'time out' at some time in their lives, whether you were sent to your room as a child for having a temper tantrum or you got the cold shoulder from a friend for interrupting a private conversation. There are two critical aspects to a time out: 1) the dog must be in an environment where he cannot find any sources of reward; and 2) he must have been anticipating a reward in the environment where he misbehaved. These conditions can be accomplished by removing the dog from the situation or removing the dog's source of reward. For instance, you come home from work and your dog greets you eagerly at the door. At some point during the jubilant reunion, he jumps on you. You immediately step outside and close the door in your dog's face. The anticipated reward for the dog was your attention. The instant he misbehaved by jumping up, you removed his reward (you). If this is done consistently, the dog will learn that jumping up on you causes you to go away. It usually makes more sense to remove yourself from the situation than to remove the dog because removing the dog is often impractical.

Maybe you have observed a time out in action among your own dogs. Puppies learn to modulate the strength of their play bites through the reaction of their playmates. One puppy bites too hard and the playmate yelps and runs away to hide for a few seconds. Play, which was the reward for both the biter and the 'bitee,' stops. The biter soon learns that by biting softly, play continues, but hard biting causes the play to cease. Likewise, my young dog learned to alter his tugging behaviour through negative punishment. Normally when he plays tug with another dog, he bites his way up the toy and tugs very close to his playmate's mouth. When playing with one particular dog, he learned to modify this intimidating behaviour because every time his mouth got too close, the dog got nervous and dropped the toy. The timid dog was timing him out for bad behaviour by removing his reward—the game. If he wanted to play tug, he had to play by the other dog's rules.

Time out is often misused. In the real life examples in the previous paragraph, the puppy or dog learned to inhibit the unwanted behaviour because the play resumed shortly after the time out. When people use time out with their dogs, they often leave the dog in a time out for such a long time that the dog does not resume the same activity. For instance, the puppy bites you too hard during play and you leave the room or place the puppy in a crate. This only works as a learning tool if you return to the puppy within a few seconds and engage in play again. It does little to leave the puppy for such a long time that he either falls asleep or becomes involved in doing something else. You want him to learn to play appropriately, which means you must engage him in play again so he can learn to inhibit the biting behaviour. Research with children also confirms that short time outs are more effective than long time outs. Time out with dogs should last two to thirty seconds. Longer than this and the dog will simply learn to amuse himself. I advise owners to use a kitchen timer so they don't forget the dog in a time out and unintentionally render it ineffective.

Why negative punishment?

Why would you choose to use negative rather than positive punishment? Both types of punishment are effective with most unwanted behaviour. However, negative punishment procedures typically take longer. With the overwhelming popularity of training methods that emphasize positive reinforcement, many owners and trainers are more comfortable with procedures that do not involve aversive control. The most compelling reason for me to consider negative punishment is that I don't want to run the risk of damaging my relationship with my dogs by scolding, shouting, or making unpleasant physical contact with them. Negative punishment procedures were developed for use with children because parents and teachers were seeking kinder, gentler ways to teach. Our dogs should be accorded the same consideration.

THE GREAT TRAINING DEBATE

Rewards or Corrections?

The world of dog training has experienced a major shift in philosophy. In the past twenty years or so, more and more dog trainers who used to depend upon corrective methods have discovered the power of positive reinforcement. And many who have come to abhor the use of corrections have polarized themselves from those trainers who feel corrections are a useful, and sometimes necessary, component of training.

I believe the controversy among dog trainers boils down to one question: "Should we use corrections with dogs and, if so, when?" The purpose of a correction is to discourage the dog from engaging in a specific behaviour. This can be accomplished through negative punishment, which involves manipulating rewards, or through positive punishment, which involves manipulating aversive events (corrections). Imagine that you wish to teach your dog not to jump up when greeting a person. A negative-punishment procedure could consist of reinforcing with treats or social contact whenever the dog sits to greet someone, and 'timing out' the dog by staring at the ceiling whenever it jumps up. A positive-punishment procedure could consist of reinforcing with treats or social contact whenever the dog sits to greet someone and administering a sharp tug downwards with a leash and training collar whenever the dog jumps up. In theory, both procedures can work.

Which procedure is 'best'?

There is no easy answer to this question because you can base your opinion on scientific evidence, ethical considerations, or both.

There are many methods of negative punishment for discouraging a dog's misbehaviour:

- differential reinforcement of behaviours other than the 'bad' behaviour

- removal of any form of reinforcement for the bad behaviour (extinction)

- imposing a cost, in terms of rewards, to the dog for engaging in the bad behaviour

- banning the dog for a short time to a time out area for engaging in the bad behaviour.

The main limitation of these methods is that the trainer must be able to systematically control the various types of reinforcement that are available to the dog. Although negative punishment can be extremely effective, there is always a time lag between implementing a negative-punishment procedure and the decrease in the occurrence of the bad behaviour. Also, these methods rarely completely eliminate behaviour from the dog's repertoire.

Procedures which use positive punishment consist of presenting some sort of aversive event for each doggy transgression. Commonly used corrections include leash pops, scruff shakes, water mist, citronella spray, a bonk with a rolled-up towel, loud noise and electric shock. The effectiveness of positive punishment is highly influenced by how the method is implemented. For instance, more intense corrections, delivered immediately after each and every display of the bad behaviour, work best. Positive punishment is always more effective if 1) you can ensure the dog is unable to escape or avoid the correction 2) if you can remove whatever causes the dog for engaging in the bad behaviour and 3) if you can provide reinforcement for engaging in 'good' behaviours in the same context.

The primary benefit of using aversive control to eliminate misbehaviour is that, in some cases, you can expect to achieve complete and permanent suppression of the bad behaviour rapidly. This is especially true when using very intense corrections. On the other hand, there are significant risks associated with the use of corrections, especially intense ones. A dog will often display emotional reactions, most notably fear, that may block the learning of appropriate behaviours. The dog will sometimes redirect aggression toward something else in the environment (another person or dog). Some dogs actually learn to be aggressive in order to *escape or avoid corrections*.

However, the most serious side effects of positive punishment involve the trainer. Because positive punishment can work so completely and so quickly, its use can become addictive to the trainer and, thus, it becomes the method of choice. And, even worse, if the corrections are not delivered properly and their effects monitored continuously, training easily becomes abusive.

Are corrections justified?

Whether or not corrections are justified is an ethical question. All trainers should certainly adhere to the Do No Harm rule. Trainers should deplore the use of any punishment procedure that causes excessive physical pain, tissue damage, lengthy or serious illness, or severe stress. *Brutal and inhumane treatment is never justified.*

An ethical trainer will weigh the risks and benefits of using aversive control carefully and compassionately. In no case should the correction be more severe than the behaviour it's designed to correct. Positive punishment, if it's going to work, will alter behaviour quickly. This allows a conscientious trainer to estimate how many corrections a dog is expected to receive and judge if this is warranted.

Special-needs children who are unable to voice their own wishes and desires are assigned advocates to represent their best interests. These advocates are sometimes faced with deciding if positive punishment is justified for dealing with serious behaviour problems. Most advocacy groups subscribe to the Principle of the Least Intrusive Alternative, which states that the least aversive method *that is expected to succeed* is always the treatment of choice. I believe this is an excellent guiding principle that trainers and behaviourists should adopt when considering the use of punishment for dogs.

Using corrections humanely: A proposal

Conscientious and educated trainers can make judicious use of short-term, well-designed and monitored programs that include corrections. However, I propose that positive punishment *only* be used in very specific circumstances. Training tends to involve either establishing good behaviours or eliminating bad ones. If the main objective of the training exercise is to establish a desirable behaviour, such as sit, down, or come, reward-based methods consisting of positive reinforcement and negative punishment should be the method of choice.

Occasionally such training will fail and, *provided the behaviour is not one of critical importance,* my recommendation is to advise the owner that the dog simply isn't capable of learning this behaviour but that he can live without it. As an example, most owners really can live with a dog that pulls on the leash—it's annoying, but not life-threatening.

There are typically only two critically important behaviours that will keep dogs safe in most environments and enhance their quality of life: come and stay. If reward-based methods don't work for these two behaviours, corrections may be warranted.

When it comes to eliminating bad behaviours, I categorize them into nuisance behaviours and dangerous behaviours. Nuisance behaviours should always be eliminated through negative punishment. If this fails, corrections may be considered *only* if the owner finds it impossible to live with the dog.

Dangerous behaviours, on the other hand, jeopardize the safety of people, other animals or the dog itself. In most cases, even dangerous behaviours can be safely controlled while negative-punishment methods are attempted. However, occasionally you may be faced with a dangerous behaviour that is not easily managed. In such a case, positive punishment, with its potential for quick and complete elimination of a behaviour, can *sometimes* save a dog from euthanasia.

No easy answers

As with many contentious issues, there are no easy answers to the great training debate. As the guardians of dogs, it's our responsibility to ensure their humane treatment and well-being. However, in very specific circumstances, the humane use of corrections may be a necessary part of teaching dogs to function in our society. This is the point where science, ethics, and dogs meet.

Part Three

BEHAVIOUR
PROBLEMS

I've had some awesome instructors when it comes to working with behaviour problems. My first teacher was Rael, a cocky little Yorkshire terrier who never mastered the concept of eliminating outside. Thanks to my dedicated efforts to teach her, she did learn to 'fake pee' in the yard, though, in anticipation of earning a treat! And some years later came Shaahiin, my beloved Saluki. Shaahiin was about the smartest dog I've ever known but he was a dedicated car chaser. Until I got the car chasing under control, I lived in constant dread that he was going to be killed. Then there was Ciaran, my thunder-phobic Border Collie. Ciaran was also fearfully aggressive with people, most often children. Eejit, a Border-Border, was the next addition to our family—ideal in every way except that he developed such a hatred for dogs that it almost ended his agility career. Eejit taught me a very valuable lesson: some behaviour problems are easier to manage than resolve. And then came my dearest Fidget. Fidget is the dog I adopted from the ASPCA shelter in New York City. She is the most well-rounded yet when it comes to behaviour problems: poor emotional regulation; noise phobic; performance anxiety; fearfully aggressive toward some strangers and most dogs; possessive of food and chewies; and downright irritable with people when she gets upset about something. And of course, like many shelter dogs, she was absolutely perfect when I first brought her home. The true Fidget didn't emerge until I'd already fallen hopelessly in love with her!

I spent many years consulting with dog owners while running my house-call practice in Toronto. I soon learned that behaviour problems are in the eye of the beholder. Sometimes people would seek my advice for the most easily managed or mundane concerns, such as jumping on the kitchen counters or barking at the postal worker. These same owners would sometimes admit that the dog regularly guarded its food or eliminated in the house, but they weren't concerned with those behaviours. Most of the behaviour problems I dealt with were normal doggy behaviours that the owners found annoying or inconvenient. Others were far from normal—some of those dogs were seriously disturbed! Those were the ones that kept me challenged. Throughout all the cases, I tried to stay true to one basic tenet: don't ask clients to do what I wouldn't do myself. And I knew what I would and wouldn't do because I'd had my share of problems with my own dogs.

While the stories that I tell in this section are fictitious, they are based on real dogs and their people. For more indepth guidance on diagnosing and treating behaviour problems, refer to these books:

- Suzanne Hetts's *Pet Behavior Protocols.*

- Karen Overall's *Clinical Behavioral Medicine for Small Animals.*

- Steven Lindsay's *Handbook of Applied Dog Behavior and Training, Vol. 2 and 3.*

- Victoria Voith and Peter Borchelt's *Readings in Companion Animal Behavior.*

- Gary Landsberg, Wayne Hunthausen & Lowell Ackerman's *Handbook of Behavior Problems of the Dog and Cat.*

- John Wright's *The Dog Who Would be King: Tales and Surprising Lessons from a Pet Psychologist.*

- Any books or material by Patricia McConnell

Nothing in Life Should be Free

Developing a Loving Bond with Your Dog Does Not Mean Catering to His Every Whim

If you ever find yourself visiting my sister, you'll be asked not to sit on the futon because it belongs to the dog. The dog is a small, black Pug named Windsor. Windsor—who is cute as a bug—has a tough life. He spends his days napping, playing and gaining weight. When he wants a snack he waddles to his 'all-you-can-eat' bowl in the kitchen. His basket of toys is placed nearby so he can grab a stuffed bear at his leisure. My sister describes Windsor as "moody"—he sometimes growls and snaps at my brother-in-law for no good reason and he has to be sedated to have his nails clipped by the veterinarian. Windsor turns into a complete demon if he gets his paws on a chew bone and he becomes a whirling dervish at my parents' home, while my sister looks on, helpless to reform his behaviour. And although he appears totally devoted to her, Windsor recoiled in fear when my sister reached out to hug him at the airport after an absence of only seven days. His allegiance had completely switched over to his dog-sitter.

No more something for nothing

Is Windsor a problem dog? Not according to my sister. But the way I see it, their relationship could be vastly improved with a few simple changes. He has too much autonomy—he has been permitted to run rampant and do as he pleases, all in the name of love.

If I had my druthers, I would place Windsor on a 'nothing-in-life-is-free' (NILIF) program. By this I mean I would determine the things that Windsor considers important in his life, such as food, toys, his futon and attention, and make his access to these contingent upon certain behaviour. If Windsor wants to go out, Windsor sits first. If Windsor wants his dinner, Windsor does a down-stay first. If Windsor wants to be cuddled, Windsor rolls over and shows his tummy first, and so on. This program can be effective for adult dogs in need of an 'attitude adjustment' and for puppies learning to bond with their human family.

Co-dependants anonymous

Some professional behaviourists and trainers advocate a NILIF program for dogs displaying aggression toward people, arguing that the act of doling out resources reinforces the dog's subordinate position. That is one possible interpretation of the effect of earning the good things in life, but I view it differently. I think NILIF works because the dog and owner become co-dependants. Controlling a dog's favourite things helps to establish a strong partnership between the dog and the owner. The dog learns to depend upon and trust the owner, and the owner learns to become attuned to the dog's needs. The goal is not to remove the dog's control but rather to teach him a new way of controlling—he learns to 'play' the owner in a mannerly fashion.

The foundation block of a strong bond

Although I admit my laxity when it comes to controlling my adult dogs' resources, when I bring a new puppy into my family, I become quite compulsive. I start scheming right away to convince the pup that I have special magical powers that cause great things to happen. Think of the Far Side cartoon that depicts the dog marveling at his owner—he drives up to a fast food window and hamburgers are passed into the car!

I begin by teaching the pup that he 'scores' every time he looks at me. He might get a piece of kibble, a special tidbit, a quick game with a toy, or an affectionate cuddle. After a day or two of this, the pup is incredibly attentive to me. Trainer Chris Bach takes this one step further—she advocates teaching the puppy that he never gets anything he wants by looking directly at it—he only gets what he wants by staring at her.

Hand feeding is another important component of NILIF. I enjoy the special moments sharing in one of the pup's favourite activities of the day, and the pup comes to view me as his very own vending machine! Sometimes the puppy just has to look at me for a piece of kibble—sometime the meal becomes a short training session. Hand-feeding has the added benefit of helping a pup feel comfortable with people around him while he's eating.

I also spend a great deal of time playing, doing my best to mimic puppy play so I will become the pup's preferred play partner. I wrestle, play-bite (gently!), tug, chase and play keep away. Gradually, I incorporate simple training exercises so the puppy thinks that learning and playing are one and the same.

A powerful bond is established between the puppy and the owner by controlling a variety of resources, not just food.

You get what you pay for

We've all heard the old adage that people don't value things that come too easily. Animals appear to be the same. When Windsor was a puppy, I gave my sister a selection of toys, including a Buster Cube, a Kong, and a Goodie Ship. She was horrified that I expected Windsor to 'work' for his food and politely returned the gifts.

Do dogs become resentful if asked to perform for their food or other needs? Some adult dogs may have trouble with the transition, but almost all come to enjoy the extra challenge. There have been numerous studies that offer animals a choice between free food and food that includes a cost. Hens will peck a key for grain and rats will press a bar for Cheerios, even though the same food is available for free, simply because they like the activity of working. Squirrels, given a choice of shelled peanuts or peanuts still in the shells, overwhelmingly prefer the latter. The squirrels find it enjoyable just handling the shells and digging out the nuts. Maybe this explains the popularity of crab and lobster for the human palate! Progressive zoos and farms enrich the environments of their animals by providing simulated foraging activities, such as giving bears salmon frozen in large blocks of ice and lions meat chunks in paper-mache piñatas.

You scratch my back and I'll scratch yours

My sister doesn't view Windsor as a problem dog because she doesn't ask much of him. That's okay. But many owners would find Windsor's aggression unacceptable, his unruly behaviour alarming and his fickle attachment disconcerting. Many of us want more from our companions. NILIF isn't a cure-all for all relationship woes between a dog and his owner, but it can contribute to the development of a new and healthy partnership. I may not win the case with my sister but I'm convinced there is a well-mannered, charming Pug inside Windsor, just clamouring to come out and play.

DOING IT RIGHT
FROM THE START

Ten Stupid Ways in Which People
Mess Up Their Dogs

Raising a puppy strikes me as being a lot like bringing up a child—a good parent provides the child with a solid foundation of education and experience. The ideal child is friendly, respectful to others, displays appropriate social behaviour and good manners, and has sufficient intelligence and knowledge to survive in the world. Most of us want the same virtues in our dogs but we have a very short time frame in which to do the job. Unlike the human child, a puppy transforms into an adult in just a few months.

Many behaviour problems can be prevented by doing things right from the start. If only every puppy could arrive at its new home, complete with a 'how-to' manual and a private tutor to ensure the job is accomplished properly! So, in the tradition of Dr. Laura Schlesinger and her *Ten Stupid Things People Do* books, here's my list of pet peeves.

1. The owner fails to provide sufficient socialization with people.
Walking a cute puppy around the neighborhood tends to work like a magnet and attract zillions of people. However, owners tell me they discourage their puppies from interacting with people because the puppy still jumps up and the owner doesn't want to deal with the embarrassment of apologizing to complete strangers. I also see owners pulling the puppy away because he is trying to make contact with an unreceptive person. In both cases, the puppy learns that it's not very reinforcing to say hello to strangers and the owner may

unintentionally teach the puppy to dislike or distrust unfamiliar people. If your puppy loves people and wants to socialize, promote it! Allow him to greet people. (Teach him to sit for greetings, of course.) And when you encounter people who don't want to say hello to your pup, it's best to distract the puppy with treats and get his attention on you rather than dragging and pulling him away from the target of his affections.

2. The owner fails to provide sufficient socialization with dogs.

The majority of puppies start out life enjoying the company of other dogs. After all, they've just spent a few months whooping it up with their littermates. Now in their new home, every time they see a dog and try to approach, the owner pulls in the other direction. You want to encourage your puppy's sociable nature and never, ever punish or frustrate your puppy by pulling him away from other dogs. Draw the puppy's attention away with treats or toys if the puppy wants to approach an unfriendly dog.

3. The owner fails to take advantage of opportunities for learning.

Puppies are little learning machines, soaking up information about how the world works. They learn some things, such as bite inhibition, coming when called and elimination on cue, more easily as puppies than as adults. Young puppies even have a following response—a built-in walk-nicely-on-leash behaviour. In a new environment, they follow wherever you go. Take advantage of this innate tendency and teach the puppy to follow your lead. Make frequent trips to new areas (safe areas where he can be off-leash) so he will be less confident. Walk away from him—he'll follow. Reward him with goodies when he does. The problem with leash training a puppy is that a leash teaches him that no matter where he goes, the owner is always about six feet behind.

4. The owner fails to provide for natural behaviours.

Owners need to recognize that the puppy is a dog, not a furry human baby. Dogs are different from people and they like to do different things. They like to explore the world with their mouths and, when they're not sleeping, they like to play *all the time*. Most puppies like to play tug, shred things, and be chased. By all means, teach them how to play these games; however, they should be taught what is and isn't appropriate. Instead of allowing the puppy to play tug with your trousers, redirect him to a tug toy. Instead of allowing the puppy to shred your shoes, redirect him to his own second-hand stuffed toys. Instead of allowing the puppy to always run away from you in play, teach him to enjoy both being chased and chasing so he can learn to come when called.

5. The owner fails to bond with the puppy through play.

In my puppy classes, I used to include a competition to see which owner, without using toys or food, could get their puppy to wag his tail the hardest. I switched tactics when I discovered that many owners have no idea how to play with their puppies. Wonderful relationships develop between puppies and owners who share playtime. Play is one way puppies learn and it should be a special activity that you share together.

6. The owner fails to handle or touch the puppy sufficiently.

Puppies need to learn to like being handled, touched, groomed, and restrained. This is not something that comes naturally to all puppies. For instance, a puppy should be taught to enjoy being held on his back to have his tummy rubbed and his feet tickled. Eventually, you will be able to use this position to clip his nails. Massage the puppy all over his body. You want him to learn that human hands are good. Regular touch is an excellent way to monitor a puppy's health, as well.

7. The owner encourages food guarding through benign neglect.

It is shocking how often I hear the mistaken belief that you shouldn't bother a dog while he's eating because he's supposed to guard his food bowl. Nonsense! Become intimately involved in your puppy's mealtime. Sit and talk with him, stroke him, and feed him his kibble by hand. Teach him to enjoy having you sit with him while he eats by giving him goodies from a stash of very special treats that are far better than what he has in his bowl. You should also make the same effort whenever the puppy has a chew bone: hold it for him so it's easier to chew, and give him special treats when you approach him while he's chewing. If he has a Kong stuffed with food, show him how talented you are because you can get the stuffing out with your fingers!

8. The owner fails to use the right balance of discipline and leniency

I see many owners who are too hard with their puppies. The owner expects the pup to behave like an adult dog and because this is impossible, ends up punishing the puppy frequently. On the other hand, I see owners who are too lenient with their puppies. The puppy has no opportunity to learn boundaries to his behaviour. A puppy needs fair and consistent rules. To paraphrase Dr. Laura and her approach to child-rearing: "A good parent provides the child with lots of love, security, respect, awe, and just a little touch of fear." While it's important for a puppy to learn that discipline will be the result if he seriously transgresses, it's the owner's responsibility to ensure the puppy knows what is expected of him before discipline ever enters the picture.

9. The owner fails to provide the puppy with sufficient exercise.

Most puppies don't get sufficient exercise. Neither do most adult dogs for that matter. We selected our various breeds to perform a variety of jobs for us, almost all of which required strenuous work. Now we expect our dogs to live in high-rise apartments and exercise by walking around a city block. Many behaviour problems can be prevented or diminished simply by providing your dog with adequate exercise. Puppies need plenty of exercise, but it needs to be on their own terms. They must be able to flop down and rest when necessary because they are still developing physically. So save the bicycle or treadmill workouts for the mature dog.

10. The owner provides the puppy with too much free food.

Owners who provide their puppies with easy access to an abundance of food are giving away a valuable tool for establishing the bond between owner and puppy. The puppy should view the owner as a food-vending machine. Get outside, even in the dead of winter, and take your cookies or kibbles along so that every time your pup looks at you, give him a treat. You will both be healthier and happier for it.

Raising a personable puppy

Raising a puppy correctly is a time consuming business with little room for error. Puppies very quickly become difficult-to-control adolescents, if they haven't been taught good manners. Sadly, many of these 'teenager' dogs end up in shelters and with breed rescue groups. A concerted effort when the pup is young can make a huge difference to the dog for the remainder of his life. Educate your fellow puppy owners and warn them about these common mistakes.

The Dog Owner's Work is Never Done
Continued Socialization is Essential to Stabilize Good Temperament

When I rang the doorbell, I heard the cacophony of barking from within. Upon entering the large suburban home, I was greeted by a beautiful Briard named Maggie and her owner, Mike. However, there was something wrong the picture. This was no typical Briard. Maggie positioned herself behind Mike and, from his shadow, she barked and growled at me. Her tail was tightly tucked up by her belly.

When I tossed a few treats at Maggie, she stopped barking and sniffed around on the floor to find them. As soon as the treats were gone, she began barking again. I stepped toward her and she backed away, still barking and growling. Once I was seated, she calmed down a bit and stopped barking but she watched me intently from her spot next to Mike's chair, growling just enough to keep me from relaxing.

Mike was totally frustrated and confused by Maggie's behaviour. He had done his research before choosing the breed. Maggie's breeder had come highly recommended by other Briard breeders and owners. He had met Maggie's dam and sire and found them friendly and well behaved. He visited the litter numerous times and the breeder helped him pick a healthy pup with a balanced temperament. Maggie went home to live with Mike at eight weeks of age. It was August.

Maggie's puppyhood

Maggie proved to be everything Mike wanted. As a puppy, she was playful, smart, and affectionate. Maggie's breeder provided Mike with important information on nutrition, grooming, and training. Mike took two weeks off work to spend time with his new puppy. He taught her to enjoy spending time in her crate, he taught her to play without biting, and he taught her to walk properly on a leash. Each day, they played in the park with two other puppies in the neighborhood.

When Maggie was 11 weeks old, he enrolled her in a puppy kindergarten class that emphasized lure-reward training methods. The instructor incorporated off-leash play sessions for the puppies and encouraged everyone, including the children, to handle the puppies. Maggie was confident and friendly with other puppies, with children, and with adults. Mike was thrilled!

Maggie's adolescence

In the fall, when Maggie was five months old, Mike changed jobs. He accepted a new position that required longer hours at the office. Maggie spent a lot of time alone. Mike left early and came home late. To his credit, he took his lunchtime off to play with Maggie in the yard. He walked her to the park each evening, but they didn't stay long because the park was always deserted that late at night. Besides, the winter evenings were getting very cold.

The first warm weekend in the spring, Mike's company held a picnic. Employees were encouraged to bring their families, including dogs. Mike proudly led Maggie over to the group, whereupon she hid behind him, barking and growling at everyone. When a curious child approached to say, "Hello," Maggie's eyes widened and she snapped at the little girl. Fortunately, no contact was made. Mike was shocked and more than a bit embarrassed. He'd bragged to everyone about Maggie, the wonder dog. Muttering something about her not feeling well, he excused himself and took Maggie home.

What went wrong?

What could possibly have caused Maggie to switch from a well-adjusted puppy to a frightened and alarming adult? Mike had done everything right with Maggie, hadn't he? She had been well-bred, well-socialized and well-trained. What went wrong?

Puppies go through an important phase in their development where they need to be exposed to all types of unfamiliar people and dogs in all sorts of locations. Research tells us that if puppies do not receive this exposure during the sensitive socialization period, it is extremely difficult, if not impossible, for the dog ever to be comfortable in new situations or friendly with strangers. However, this is not the complete story.

It's true that socialization during those early months is the *necessary first step* in ensuring a solid temperament. However, *continued* socialization throughout adolescence is essential for the dog to stabilize that temperament. Locking the teenage Maggie up for the winter while Mike attended to his professional responsibilities basically erased much of the effort he had put into Maggie when she was a puppy.

Repairing the damage

Incompletely socialized dogs sometimes bounce back with a bit of effort. Some never seem to regain the confidence they once had. Fortunately, Maggie was resilient. Mike first adjusted his work schedule to spend more time with Maggie. He arranged to have people visit daily. The guests brought her special treats and toys to teach her that visits are a positive experience. He did not, however, force Maggie to undergo petting—she merely had to stay in the same room to enjoy the goodies.

Mike also took Maggie for walks every day. He made it easy at first by taking her to quiet areas where she would see only a few people and then gradually venturing on to more heavily populated streets. He gave Maggie treats every time they passed someone until she began to anticipate the reward and look to Mike whenever a person approached. He discouraged people from petting her until she stopped clinging to him and began to wag her tail at passersby.

Lastly, Mike got Maggie involved in agility training to boost her confidence. She was first introduced to the obstacles in private lessons but quickly progressed to group classes as she began to enjoy the game.

The agility training proved to be the final step that helped Maggie overcome her fears. She began to associate people and dogs with an activity she really enjoyed—in no time at all, she became very comfortable with new people. Mike is really looking forward to this year's company picnic!

HOUSETRAINING
BLUES

What to Do if Your Dog Refuses to Eliminate Outdoors

These dog owners were singing the blues and the chorus went something like this: "Help! We can't housetrain our new dog!" Susie, an eight month old female Beagle, was urinating and defecating in the house. In fact, Susie resolutely refused to eliminate outside. The owners tried going for very long walks. They hung out at the park. Susie would hold it until she got back home, then find a nice quite spot in the basement to deposit her wastes. Susie had been adopted just a few weeks before from a local animal shelter. Her history was unknown.

Susie's story is not a common one. Fortunately, most dogs are relatively easy to teach to eliminate outside. They usually prefer to go somewhere away from their sleeping, eating and playing areas. To further help along the process, many dogs use their urine for scent marking, and so the scent of other dogs prompts them to eliminate outside.

Puppies, at about seven to nine weeks of age, develop a preference for eliminating on familiar substrates. If they are regularly placed on grass to eliminate, they will prefer grass. If placed on gravel, they will prefer gravel. If exposed to a variety of substrates, just about anything is acceptable. My five month old puppy had no trouble making the adjustment to void on pavement after our move to Manhattan, but my older dog simply held it until he could find the occasional postage stamp sized bit of vegetation! This tendency to want to use a familiar substrate is one reason why I discourage paper-training in puppies. Most owners want their dog to go outside, so establish that preference right from the start. I also think it must be confusing for a puppy to first learn that eliminating inside the house is okay and then changing the rules when the dog gets older.

Writing the verses

There are a number of plausible explanations for how Susie came to avoid eliminating outdoors. It's possible that Susie had not been taken out as a youngster and, as a result, she has a preference for eliminating on carpet.

The most expedient way to resolve this is to completely restrict Susie's access to her preferred substrate and take her outside at very frequent intervals until she finally eliminates. The owner can encourage Susie to drink plenty of water (play "bobbing for treats") so she will experience a strong need to urinate. Continue to take her to the same place each time so the familiar odours will stimulate her.

A second possibility is that the owners are setting themselves up for failure. A dog will learn quickly to withhold elimination if that leads to prolonged walks. Susie's owners may have inadvertently taught her to hold her waste simply by ending the walk as soon as the job is done.

This problem can be resolved by taking Susie to the same area at the beginning of each outing and *waiting* until she eliminates before going for a walk. As soon as she urinates or defecates, immediately say, "Okay let's go," and then take her for at least a ten minute walk. If Susie doesn't produce at the peeing post in the allotted time, there should be no walk. However, her owners must make absolutely sure that Susie does not have the opportunity to eliminate inside if they return without walking.

A third explanation is that in Susie's earlier life, she may well have been severely punished for accidents in the house. In her confusion, Susie might have learned not to eliminate in front of people to avoid punishment. So, reluctant to eliminate on walks with the owners present, she opts to sneak off by herself at the first opportunity back home.

Another scenario is that being outside is so stimulating to Susie that she cannot relax to eliminate. She waits until she gets back to the less stimulating home environment.

My Border Collie would rarely defecate at the park because that was the place to play Frisbee. He didn't want to lose a moment of Frisbee playing so he always waited until we got back home. But I'm pleased to report that once there, he always did his business in the yard.

When I observed Susie, it was clear that she was too frightened on walks to engage in a vulnerable activity like elimination. She was hyper vigilant—constantly on the lookout for danger, and elimination was the last thing on her mind. The solution was to find a comfortable, quiet yard so she could learn to eliminate there, while at the same time, address her fear of the hustling, bustling city.

To crate or not to crate?

Confinement helps the housetraining process because dogs are reluctant to soil their sleeping area unless they've been forced to do so and, thus, have overcome their natural aversion.

The dog is kept in a small area—such as a crate—for a period of time and then taken directly outside to eliminate. If the dog voids outside, he can be given time out of the crate with little risk of an accident. At some point, the dog is either taken outside or placed back in the crate again. The dog is taken outside on a frequent regular schedule. If he doesn't eliminate on an outing, he's back in the crate until the next opportunity. The crate is used, not as punishment for failure to eliminate, but rather as a means to prevent the dog from eliminating inside.

While crating can facilitate housetraining, it can also be a tool of abuse. Dogs should not be kept crated for long periods of time without sufficient exercise and opportunities for socialization with people.

Puppies may be able to sleep all night in a crate without getting outside to eliminate but, during the day, a puppy should not be crated for more hours than its age in months, plus one. In other words, a two month old puppy should not be crated longer than three hours and a five-month-old puppy should be crated no more than six hours at a time. A housetraining crate should be only large enough for the puppy or dog to lie in comfortably. If too large, the pup might learn to eliminate at one end and sleep at the other.

The use of a crate is not essential for housetraining. Some owners prefer to tether the dog to them (the umbilical cord technique), which also serves to discourage the dog from eliminating because he's restricted to a small area. Tethering also enables the owner to observe the dog constantly for cues that he needs to void.

Confinement is really only necessary when the dog cannot be watched. If you have no other demands on your time and you can devote yourself to watching your dog like a hawk, you can easily accomplish housetraining. In fact, someone once advised me that the fastest way to housetrain a puppy is to install brand-new white carpeting in your home. You'll be completely committed to ensuring the pup never has an accident!

When disaster strikes

A puppy or dog must learn two things to be fully housetrained: 1) it is pleasant to eliminate outside; and 2) it is unpleasant to eliminate inside. Some puppies develop such a strong surface preference that they have only one or two accidents and never look back. Most, however, have a few disasters in the house before they figure out that going inside is not a good idea.

For the pup to learn expediently, it's a good idea for the owner to respond immediately at the first sight or sound of the puppy eliminating inside. My natural reaction is to shriek, which works well because most dogs are startled and stop in mid-flow the instant they hear me! I grab the poor puppy and race outside with him to the toilet area. Within a few seconds, he can finish what he started and in this context, I praise and reward him. So, in one instance, the pup learns two very different consequences for eliminating inside versus out.

"Hurry up and go!"

Many owners enjoy the pleasure of a dog that eliminates on cue. Teaching a dog to void on cue is relatively easy, provided you can take him to the same spot each time he needs to go. As you near the spot, say your special cue words ("hurry up" is a popular choice) and wait for the dog to eliminate. The words become associated with the dog's imminent release of wastes so that eventually, the words themselves trigger the need to void.

When the dog does urinate or defecate, praise and reward with a treat, or do something else the dog enjoys, such as going for a walk or playing a favourite game, like fetch.

My dog learned to urinate on cue at flyball tournaments. He desperately wants to go inside to race but I require that he urinate first. Now he sometimes tries to fake me out by lifting his leg without actually producing anything in his haste to get back inside!

"Help! I need out!"

Most dogs figure out for themselves how to ask to go outside when they need to eliminate. They bark, they whine, they scratch at the door, they become restless and paw at the owner. Other dogs never learn and the owner is always trying to read the dog's mind. Such dogs can be taught to ask. The first step is to teach the behaviour you want the dog to do, such as paw at the door, bark or ring a bell. Teach this response until the dog will perform it on cue. The second step is to teach the dog to perform this behaviour when he wants outside. I take the dog to the door, show him a treat or his favourite toy, and place it outside. I close the door and then cue the dog to bark or paw. As soon as he does, I reward him by opening the door so he can get the treat or toy. I repeat this many times until the dog performs the behaviour without my asking him. Then I generalize the training by cueing him to perform the behaviour whenever he needs or wants outside. Most dogs learn this lesson quickly.

No more singing the blues

Susie quickly learned that it was safe to eliminate in a quiet secluded corner of the yard. Once the owners started restricting Susie's ability to wander about the house unsupervised, the incidence of accidents dropped to nil. Over the next several months, Susie became more comfortable with city life and started to relax and enjoy her walks. Coincident with this, she began urinating, and then defecating, at the park. Eventually, Susie's owners were able to forego the excursions to the yard, as elimination outside became intrinsically reinforcing to Susie. No more housetraining blues!

HUSH, PUPPY!

Controlling Canine Noise Pollution

A troop of angry neighbors marched down the street toward the home of the little red Cocker Spaniel. Everyone in the community knew this dog because, since the family moved in, the dog has made its presence known by barking non-stop! Excessive barking is a common behaviour problem that results in frustrated owners and irate neighbors. If you were the owner of the Cocker, what would you do???

Why dogs bark

Dogs vocalize (they bark, they whine, they howl, they 'talk') for many reasons—dogs bark to defend their territory, they bark to alert you to something exciting, they bark for your attention, they bark to communicate their wants and needs, they bark when other dogs bark, they bark when anxious and upset, they bark when aroused and frustrated, they bark to warn others they are feeling aggressive, they bark to entertain themselves, they bark when they are bored and they bark when they are happy!

There are dramatic differences among breeds and among individual dogs in how likely they are to bark. My Saluki will bark occasionally when someone comes to the door while my terrier-mix barks at anything and everything. Small breeds and terriers are prone to sounding an alarm at every sound, whereas the guarding breeds are more likely to bark specifically when someone approaches their property. Some herding breeds, like the Border Collie, almost never bark while working stock, while other breeds, like the Shetland Sheepdog, bark to encourage the stock to move. Cocker Spaniels have been reported capable of emitting over one hundred barks per minute! With extremely vocal breeds, the owner must recognize that some amount of barking is an inevitable fact of life.

Preventing barking problems

Barking can easily become a serious problem if you're not careful. Prevention is the key. Ensure that barking does not become an established habit. Repetitive barking can seem like a compulsive behaviour and I suspect some dogs even experience a release of endorphins (a 'high') from barking. Disrupt or distract your puppy whenever he barks so the barking doesn't continue uninterrupted. Make sure he's not left on his own, unsupervised, for long periods of time. Intervene if you hear him barking in the yard. Discourage excessive barking at people or other dogs by asking the pup to do something appropriate. Reinforce quiet behaviour.

Rehabilitating the chronic barker

'Fixing' a barking problem depends upon a thorough analysis of the conditions that elicit barking. You may need to address a larger problem, for instance if you have a dog that barks or howls when left alone. Such a dog is probably suffering from separation distress and, if you treat the anxiety, the barking should diminish.

If your dog is barking because he's left for long hours in the backyard—as a result of poor house behaviour—then intensive training in household manners is the answer. If your dog rarely gets out for walks and so finds people and dogs passing by intimidating, problem barking can be decreased by exposing the dog to the real world. Then such stimulation becomes commonplace and is no cause for alarm. A careful analysis of the dog's motivation for barking will often lead to successful intervention.

The attention-seeking barker

If your dog has learned to bark for attention, you are caught in a tricky bind. If you attempt to change the rules and withhold attention when your dog barks, it will be tough going for awhile. At first, your dog will get frustrated and bark even more. This is called an extinction burst. The dog is saying, "Hey what's going on? Barking always worked before. Maybe I better try harder!" You can help the process along by teaching your dog an alternative behaviour, such as bringing you a toy (which occupies his mouth) to gain your attention, but this will take persistence on your part!

'Speaking' on command

A popular suggestion for dealing with a problem barker is to teach the dog to bark on command. The rationale is that, by placing the barking behaviour under your control, the dog will be less likely to bark when not requested to perform. I've had little success with this technique; in fact I find that often the dog barks even more! I also question the reasoning—my dogs are trained to sit on cue but that doesn't mean they are less inclined to sit when I don't ask them.

Anti-bark collars

In our high-tech world, we have electronic training devices that can be used to induce behavioural changes in dogs. Anti-bark collars are designed to activate automatically whenever the dog barks, delivering a noxious stimulus, such as a sound, a spray of citronella solution, or a mild shock.

Do these collars work? First, keep in mind that most dogs become 'collar-wise' in that the dog will cease barking only when wearing the collar. Collars that sound an alarm when the dog barks are often more annoying to the owners than to the dogs. Collars with a high-frequency sound are spectacularly ineffective for curbing barking.

The citronella spray collar, on the other hand, decreased barking in seven of nine cases examined in one study. There are a number of limitations to the citronella spray collar, though. First, dogs with heavy manes are often unperturbed by the spray as it never reaches the nose. Second, the collar relies on a microphone to pick up the sound of the dog's bark and activate the spray. In a home with more than one barking dog, the collar may discharge when either dog barks—resulting in confusion for the dog that is wearing the collar! Third, I have seen dogs that are able to outsmart the collar—they roll around until the collar moves to the back of the neck so the spray harmlessly shoots out over their head!

The shock anti-bark collar is quite effective for curbing nuisance barking, although many people find the idea of using shock on their dogs unacceptable. Quality models enable you to set the shock level appropriately for your dog, have probes that penetrate thick hair and rely on a vibration probe to activate the delivery of shock so it is not triggered by other dogs.

When would it be appropriate to use an anti-bark collar? Rarely should a collar be used as the first course of action, unless the dog's owner is about to be evicted. I prefer to see collars used only for situations in which the dog is *not* motivated by fear. Anti-bark collars are effective because the dog learns to inhibit barking to avoid the noxious stimulation. Hence, these collars are based on punishment and should not be used on a fearful dog, except as a very last resort.

It's important to assess the arousal level of the dog when considering the use of anti-bark collars. I recall a Bernese Mountain Dog that barked at people out the front window and raced back and forth along the fence line with a dog in the adjacent yard, both dogs barking ferociously. The citronella spray collar was very effective in the house, but when we put the Berner in the backyard, he charged up and down the fence with the other dog, totally oblivious to the citronella spray. He emptied the reservoir in less than a minute! Dogs that are highly aroused are unlikely to be deterred by even moderate aversive stimulation.

Canine good neighbors

As we continue to require that dogs live in increasingly more urban environments, it's critical that we make a concerted effort to curb nuisance barking in our dogs. Quiet, well-behaved dogs are canine good neighbors that contribute to harmony within the community.

FRONT DOOR ETIQUETTE

Working Around Your Dog's Territorial Behaviour

I approached the front door of the stately home with trepidation, wondering how I would be received. There was a large *Beware of Dog* sign in the window. I reached up and rang the doorbell. The instant it sounded, a volley of ferocious barks erupted from within, accompanied by the sound of thundering paws. I glanced across at the large bay window overlooking the doorway and there was the snarling face of a Soft Coated Wheaten Terrier looking back at me. I saw a hand reach out to grab the dog's collar and the dog was pulled away from the window, barking and straining. Shortly thereafter, the door opened and a harried looking woman smiled and invited me inside. I saw the dog safely barricaded behind a gate and, as I entered, he wagged his tail and gave me a friendly 'dog smile.'

Barney was in serious trouble. He was currently under quarantine after biting a courier. When the owner cracked open the door to receive a package, Barney barged past, knocked over the unsuspecting fellow, bit him on the thigh and arm, and then trotted off to urinate on the neighbour's lawn.

Although Barney had never done anything like this before, his attitude toward the postal worker who delivered the mail daily suggested that he was on the road to becoming a biter. Barney was a doting companion to Mrs. White for most of the day, following her from room to room and occasionally nudging her for attention. However, around noon each day, Barney would switch to hanging out downstairs, pacing back and forth between the door and the window, becoming more and more agitated. The slightest sound prompted Barney to growl ominously at the door. The pacing continued until the postal worker arrived, by which time Barney was primed to charge at the window repeatedly. Within a few minutes of the postal worker leaving, Barney was back to his charming self!

Barney was normally friendly to guests coming into the home. Sure, he would bark and carry on, as many dogs do, but he was never aggressive. Upon further questioning, though, I discovered that Mrs. White had just started using her home as her workplace. This was the first time she had opened the door to a courier and coincidentally, he'd come about the same time as the mail was normally delivered. Could it be that Barney, in his worked-up state, believed that the courier was his longtime adversary, the postal worker?

It's us against them

Dogs adopt an 'us against them' mentality because of their heritage. The ancestral wolf lives in family groups and each group defends a home range against wolf strangers. The benefits of defending a space are obvious—intruding wolves don't exploit sources of food in the area and don't post a threat to the pups. Many dogs display this same inclination to react with hostility to unfamiliar intruders, whether they are other dogs or people. In fact, certain guarding breeds have been genetically selected for the strength of their territorial tendencies.

In wolves, territorial behaviour appears around sixteen to twenty weeks of age, coinciding with the onset of neophobia—a heightened sensitivity to anything novel. At this age, wolf pups start exploring the world away from the den and are more likely to encounter other animals. It's not known whether dogs show signs of territorial behaviour at a comparable point in their development, but most owners seek help for their anti-social dogs between one and two years of age. Owners of territorial dogs often find themselves living like hermits because friends politely decline invitations to visit and pizza places refuse to deliver!

"It's the mailman. He scares me."

Gary Larson obviously knows dogs, judging from his cartoon of a dog, lying on the psychiatrist's couch, confessing his fear of the mailman! Territorial aggression is more likely in dogs that were not well socialized to people during development. The effect of socialization is to negate neophobic tendencies. Poorly socialized dogs are nervous and suspicious of strangers; in familiar environments, such as the home, where dogs feel more confident, this wariness may be expressed as aggression.

However, some territorially aggressive dogs don't fit this pattern. These dogs are friendly to people in virtually all situations except at the front door. As youngsters, they were too welcoming, leaping on the guests, barking and mouthing with wild abandon. Desperate owners tried to protect their guests by holding the dog back. Restraining a dog by the collar or confining the dog to a closed room before answering the door leads to frustration and, for many individuals, frustration elicits aggression.

Barney's attack on the courier was probably due to a long history of frustration. The arrival of the postal worker each day was exasperating for Barney because he could watch him from the window but was never permitted to meet him. The heightened arousal Barney experienced in anticipation of the postal worker's arrival each day further fueled the frustration, and Barney became a canine time bomb. The unsuspecting courier was simply in the wrong place at the wrong time.

Getting the bark without the bite

Most owners want a dog that barks to warn off potential intruders but they don't want a dog that bites people entering the home. Fortunately, even dogs that look forward to company coming will usually bark to announce a guest's arrival. Mrs. White's goal was for Barney to bark but not bite.

It was imperative for Barney to be managed closely during treatment so that he couldn't harm another caller. Mrs. White had already erected a gate at the bottom of the stairs that overlooked the foyer so Barney could be contained, yet still see the goings-on at the front door. This is important so as not to further increase his frustration.

Mrs. White embarked on a training program designed to replace Barney's current actions with more socially appropriate behaviour. She taught Barney to "Go to his spot" at the landing of the stairs and to stay there until he was released. This was rehearsed until Barney could stay despite all sorts of distractions, including Mrs. White opening the door and pretending to greet a visitor. If Barney moved off the landing before being released, Mrs. White used her body to block him from coming down the stairs, pushed him back into place, and then repeated the exercise. When Barney stayed in place, he was rewarded handsomely with his favorite treats, *while he was still in his spot.*

The next step was to teach Barney to go to his spot automatically when the doorbell sounded. Mrs. White had an extra button wired inside the house so she could ring the bell several times throughout the day. Barney learned to race to the door, barking up a storm, and then dash up the stairs to sit and wait for his reward. At this point, Mrs. White attached a strong leash to the banister so that when someone unfamiliar came to the door, Barney was tethered, with no chance of an error. The gate was still in place as backup.

Once Barney had learned a new set of actions to perform, it was time to transfer the behaviour to more realistic situations. Mrs. White recruited friends and family who Barney knew well to help with mock visits. She had to use familiar people so Barney would not pose a threat to the volunteers. When a friend came to the door, Barney understandably had a tough time staying in his spot. However, with persistence and *many repetitions*, he learned to go to his spot and either stay there for the entire interaction (such as when a courier dropped off a package) or stay there until invited down to meet the guest (such as when a friend came to visit). Each mock visit lasted only a few minutes, with plenty of rewards for Barney; then the volunteer would leave for five to ten minutes and return again, so Barney was able to learn from several 'visits' in one session. With each subsequent repetition, Barney was less excited and more likely to succeed.

Making the jump from familiar people to strangers took planning. Mrs. White hosted a Saturday barbecue and invited a mix of friends and people Barney did not know. Each person was asked to arrive at a specific time, arranged so that Mrs. White would have fifteen minutes to work with each guest before the next arrived. During a fifteen-minute session, the guest came to the door, Barney went through his routine, the guest left for a few minutes, then returned, and so on, until the next caller arrived. Barney's friends were scheduled to come first, and strangers arrived only after Barney had received plenty of practice. By the time unfamiliar people began showing up at the door, Barney was much less excited, and well versed in what he was to do. Furthermore, Mrs. White had plenty of friends present to help, in case Barney's training broke down with the arrival of the first stranger.

Martha Stewart's dog etiquette

Imagine one of Martha Stewart's dogs for a moment. I envision an exquisitely groomed dog that waits politely as guests are ushered into the foyer, then offers a welcoming paw when people move into the sitting room. After a brief greeting, the dog snoozes in front of the fireplace, waking only to clear the carpet of any delectable crumbs that may have fallen. Pure fantasy? Sure, but any dog can learn to be a good host.

Training in front door etiquette accomplishes two important goals. First, it teaches the dog very specific actions to perform when someone comes to the door, rather than allowing the dog to run amok. These actions also happen to be incompatible with jumping up on, charging or biting guests.

Second, it teaches the dog that good things happen when people come to visit. The dog is praised and reinforced with treats or play or whatever turns him on.

All too often, we simply assume that dogs will like people and fail to do anything to ensure that the tendency for territoriality does not overwhelm their sociability. A proactive approach to maintaining socialization and teaching proper etiquette will ensure fewer Barneys and fewer bites. Teach your dog to be a good host and make Martha Stewart proud!

AND BABY MAKES
FOUR

Most Dogs are Compliant, but Some Need Help Accepting the New Addition to the Family

We're all familiar with images of Lassie—patient guardian, frolicking playmate, and ardent protector of young master Timmy. The stuff of Hollywood legends, right? Maybe, but our vision of the perfect family often includes a loyal dog, keeping a watchful eye over the children. However, adding a baby to the family can be a trying time for the dog, especially if the dog has been the 'only child.'

Most dogs do come to view the baby as an integral part of the family, even if they may not step fully into the Lassie role. Sadly, though, some dogs become fearful or resentful of the baby and this can lead to family discord—and sometimes even disaster.

Unlikely Lassies

Expectant parents need to objectively evaluate how their dog will deal with the new family addition. There are a number of factors that contribute to disharmony between dogs and children. Dogs that behave badly toward children often do so because they have not been well socialized with children and find them unfamiliar and frightening. Children move quickly and unpredictably, they have loud, shrill voices, and their faces may be intimidating because they are at 'dog level.'

Dogs that are possessive about their food, bones, or toys, and guard them from people should not be around children until this issue has been resolved. This is because children are more likely than adults to try to take something from the dog. A dog that is normally friendly to children can still behave aggressively if the child is in the vicinity of a valued object.

Some dogs appear to react to babies like squeaky toys. The dog may be fine around the baby until it cries and wriggles, at which point the dog picks up the infant and shakes it, sometimes causing serious or even fatal injuries. Thankfully, such dogs are rare. And, to be sure, there are many dogs that shake their toys violently during play that would never display this same behaviour toward a baby. However, I'd be concerned about any dog that becomes extremely aroused and excited by a baby's cry.

Elderly or irritable dogs may not tolerate a child because of the erratic and potentially painful ways the child can interact with the dog. A dog that reacts by snapping when touched on certain areas of its body because of chronic pain is not a good candidate for living with a young child. Dogs with sensory deficits, such as deafness or blindness, can also have trouble adjusting to life with a child because of the unpredictability and chaos that children bring.

Take time to prepare

Expectant parents are wise to prepare the dog for the baby well in advance. Dogs become accustomed to routine and can be stressed when an established pattern is suddenly interrupted. If walks or training activities are going to be rescheduled or cut back, introduce the changes gradually. If some of the dog's privileges, such as getting on the bed or sitting on the owner's lap, will be curtailed, introduce those restrictions before the baby's arrival so the dog has plenty of time to adjust.

Does it help to practice with a lifelike doll? It's doubtful the dog will be fooled into believing the doll is a real baby but a doll can help the parents simulate new activities, such as feeding, carrying, rocking, etc. If possible, use clothes and blankets that smell of a young baby to get the dog used to novel odors. If the dog is inclined to jump when you lift the doll up into your arms, be sure to teach the dog to Sit or Down whenever you are handling the doll. Praise the dog for gentle contact with the doll.

Dogs that are sensitive about noises can get agitated or frightened when a baby cries. It can help to play an audiotape of baby noises while giving the dog plenty of attention, play, or treats. If the dog is afraid of the taped noises, you may need to start with the volume very low and increase it gradually as the dog learns to enjoy the experience.

Excellent verbal control of the dog is a good idea when it comes to juggling the requirements of the dog and a baby, so the pregnancy months are a good time to hone the dog's obedience skills. Certain behaviours are particularly useful, such as Sit, Down, Stay, Wait, Leave it, Come, Go, Get back, Take it, and Give.

The first meeting

Introducing the dog to the new baby can be stressful for everyone involved. It is very important to stay calm. If the parents act nervous and jumpy, the dog may become nervous as well.

If possible, come in and greet the dog first, without the baby, so the dog will be the centre of attention for a few moments. Once the dog is calm, bring the baby in. Encourage the dog to approach and sniff the baby. Distract the dog with plenty of treats so his attention is divided between the baby, the adults and the food. Intersperse with obedience exercises to keep the dog under control. Praise the dog for calm interest in the baby. You want to ensure that he has pleasant associations with the baby.

If the parents suspect that the dog might behave badly, he should be wearing a muzzle or a head halter and leash for control. He should be accustomed to this equipment before the introduction. A muzzle allows everyone to feel more relaxed and the dog can be permitted freedom of movement so he won't feel trapped in a scary situation. Begin the introduction with the dog a few feet away from the baby. Have the dog lie down and offer him treats or whatever he enjoys that is consistent with being relaxed. Talk to him reassuringly while gradually moving closer. Carefully allow him to sniff the baby. Praise him for gentle contact. If he gets agitated, end the session. Give the dog time to calm down, maybe go for a walk, and then conduct another short meeting.

Daily life with baby

As hard as it may be to implement, the strategy that works best is to pay plenty of attention to the dog when the baby is awake and to ignore him when the baby is sleeping or absent. When the baby is around, good things, such as stroking, cuddling, playing, eating treats, etc., happen for the dog. When the baby's not present, interactions with the dog are minimal. For instance, you can have the baby in your lap while you talk and stroke the dog, give treats or play fetch. Or you can give the dog a chew bone while you attend to the baby. When you feed the baby, feed the dog as well. When you walk the dog, take the baby along in a pram or baby backpack.

Before the baby is able to interact with the dog, prepare the dog for what the baby might do, such as grabbing, poking and pulling. Even though you will teach the baby to handle the dog gently, you must also teach the dog to expect, and even enjoy, 'baby moves.' Teach him that good things always follow being poked and grabbed. For instance, pull the dog's ear, say, "Oh, wasn't that fun?" and give him a treat. Then, when the baby pinches the dog's tail, you can say, "Oh, wasn't that fun?" and the dog will expect to get a treat!

You can also get your dog used to crawling before the baby becomes mobile. Dogs that have only lived with adults have never seen people crawl, so it can be an alarming and intimidating experience. Crawl toward him and give him cuddles and treats. Once he is comfortable with this new game and anticipates the treats, incorporate the baby into the picture. Place the baby on your back, supported by your partner, when you crawl. This will prepare the dog for the day the baby comes zooming in at him!

If your dog seems nervous of the baby, teach the dog to "Go away" *before* the baby starts crawling. I teach my dogs to move in the direction I gesture with my hand. You can move the dog from a distance, if you see the baby crawling toward him or if you see the dog looking uncomfortable in an interaction with the baby. Most parents routinely remove the child when the dog gets uncomfortable but this perpetuates the dog's behaviour: when he growls or snaps, the child is removed, and this reinforces the aggressive behaviour. Instead, teach him to move himself. Sometimes the dog just needs to learn that moving away is an option—if the dog feels uncomfortable about being close to the child, he can relocate elsewhere. Of course, until the dog is reliable about "Go away," in the interest of safety, remove the child!

Pay attention to the layout of the home. Some dogs are fine with the baby unless they feel trapped. Minimize the amount of furniture in the rooms or pull furniture away from the walls and corners to allow for escape routes. Teach the dog to jump over the backs or sides of chairs and sofas so he won't get trapped, should the baby pull up onto the furniture. Once the baby starts moving around, establish a safe zone for the dog. This zone should be up high where the baby can't reach and in the room where the dog spends most of his time. Use a phrase, such as "go to your spot," so the dog can be encouraged to go there when activities get hectic.

Is discipline helpful?

Despite all the best efforts of the parents, some dogs are going to growl or snap at the baby. Does it help to scold or punish the dog? While it might work for some dogs, it can also backfire because it teaches the dog to anticipate punishment whenever the child is present. If the child becomes a signal for punishment, the dog will fear or resent the child. A firm "No" may be sufficient for the dog, as a means of communicating what is unacceptable behaviour. In general, though, the best way to deal with an aggressive dog is to change his motivation for behaving aggressively. We do this by teaching the dog to like being around the child.

If you have a dog that growls, I recommend that you *do not* punish the dog for growling. This is a warning signal from the dog and, if you come down hard on him for warning, he may stop. And then you'll have no way of knowing when your dog is feeling aggressive. As long as the dog growls, you have the opportunity to remove the dog or the child from the situation.

Default behaviour

Dogs that have been aggressive to children in the past should *never* be completely trusted. Much like a computer can be set back to the factory defaults, a dog may appear totally rehabilitated but, under stress, may revert back to former behaviour patterns.

Always supervise interactions between a dog and child and always be aware of the dog's emotional state. If the dog looks worried or nervous, be especially cautious and do something to help the dog feel more comfortable.

Not every dog can play "Lassie"

Dogs and kids do go together but it takes the right kind of dog. Some dogs are simply unable to adjust to children and are happiest as 'only dogs.' Real world Lassies do exist (at least with respect to their attraction to kids) and the more you prepare your dog for life with children, the more likely you and your family can experience the Hollywood fantasy.

WHAT'S MINE IS MINE...

And What's Yours Is Mine Too!

A litter of young puppies at feeding time is a classic example of survival of the fittest. They clamber over each other, pushing and shoving to gain access to a tray of food. They behave like little pigs. And for good reason—he who gobbles the quickest gains weight the fastest! As they get older, the struggle becomes more intense. Try giving them a particularly tasty item, such as a piece of rawhide or a pig ear, and an all-out war may ensue, with snarling, squabbling and scrapping. Once the rawhide is gone, peace returns to the puppy pen.

I see the same type of behaviour all the time in my practice—the affectionate, sweet family dog who turns into a veritable monster at meal time. Sometimes the dog is locked in a room while he eats so no one inadvertently comes too close. The dog never has the pleasure of chewing a tasty bone because the family wouldn't be safe, especially if he decides to hide the bone among the sofa pillows. In a puppy, possessiveness may be considered normal and even cute. In an adult dog, possessiveness can be downright dangerous.

Preventing possessiveness in puppies

Growing up in a litter naturally leads to competition. Some puppies are more vigorous than others in their defense of food, toys and other goodies. When the puppy goes to his new home, he has no idea that things are different. At feeding time, a particularly voracious puppy will likely wolf down his food, growling and snarling if anyone comes near. Sadly, I often hear people say, "But you just don't go near a dog while it is eating. You can't do anything about that." Not true—but the earlier you intervene, the easier it is to succeed.

It's necessary to actually teach a dog not to be possessive, and puppy-hood is the best time to accomplish this. Once the dog is an adult, you have a large set of teeth with which to contend. The dog also has a long history of being successful with aggression.

One of the most important lessons a puppy can learn is that there's no reason to defend food from people. The pup needs to be taught that people can and do take food away from him, but that this is to be welcomed. The pup should be comfortable with people, especially children, around the food bowl during meals. My dogs are free to growl at each other should someone stick their nose near another's dish, but growling at me is not an issue because they have no reason to feel threatened.

One of the first things I did when I brought my new puppy home was become actively involved in his mealtimes. I sat with him, petting and tickling him—probably even annoying him a bit. When he got tense and growled, under no circumstances did I scold him or take his food away. That is absolutely the worst thing you can do. Instead, I got some really special treats, such as cooked liver. Every time I touched him, I put a piece of really tasty stuff in his bowl. What did my puppy learn from this? "Hey, whenever this new person touches me while I'm eating, she gives me something extra yummy." I also took food out of his bowl and held it in my palm so he could eat directly from my hands. Once he was comfortable and relaxed with me touching him, I switched to periodically lifting up his bowl to put a few pieces of the good stuff in. He learned that he really likes me taking his dish away because, when I give it back, it's even better. Occasionally, I placed fewer kibbles in his bowl than he needed for his meal, and then, as he ate, I added more. Also, because he was a puppy, he got smaller portions than my adult dogs and he always finished first. So he never experienced the other dogs trying to take his food from him (not that I would have permitted them to anyway).

Food bowl exercises with the puppy are extremely important, but they aren't enough. Many dogs are blasé about their regular food but will vigorously defend tasty bones they're given or forbidden food they steal. My puppy was given several different types of chew toys, including Kongs stuffed with cheese whiz or peanut butter, smelly tripe rawhides, and marrow bones. The Kongs were the large size, so there was no way he could reach to the bottom to get all the stuff out. When I saw him becoming frustrated, I'd come up and give him a 'hand,' so to speak. Reaching into the Kong with my finger, I demonstrated how helpful people can be at assisting poor puppies in need! I did the same with the marrow bones. As he worked away stretching his tongue to the limit, I showed him how I can push large amounts of the tasty goo out one end. The puppy learned to bring me his treats to hold while he works at them because I'm so clever and helpful.

Possessiveness in adult dogs

The same types of exercises can benefit the adult dog, but the owner must proceed cautiously. Often feeding by hand is a necessary starting point, with no bowl present at all. Feeding in a different room from the usual place can help set a more peaceful tone. As the dog learns to relax while being fed by hand, a new and very different looking bowl from the customary one should be introduced. At first, just have it empty, in your lap. Occasionally drop a few kibbles in it and encourage the dog to eat them while you hold the bowl. Over days, hold the bowl closer and closer to the floor while, at the same time, add kibbles or special treats as the dog eats. Once you place the bowl on the floor, realize that he may now perceive that the bowl is 'his.' However, by this point, he should be comfortable eating with you in close proximity. Practice stroking him and adding extra yummy treats to the bowl while he eats. If he's relaxed, try lifting the bowl to add the goodies. Let him watch you so he knows exactly what you are doing. Eventually, you should be able to walk around the room, occasionally returning to pet the dog or add extra food to the bowl. Only once the dog is completely relaxed with you touching him, standing close to him, and reaching down to add more food to the bowl, should you move the bowl back to the original feeding spot (if feasible, just continue to feed in the new location).

To address possessiveness of chewies, I start an adult dog with a hard, plastic bone (which isn't nearly as tasty as rawhide). I drill two holes through the bone at one end. I stuff cheese or wieners into the holes to make the bone slightly more interesting. I hold the bone by the other end and allow the dog to lick out the yummy stuff. Once the holes are empty, the bone is no longer desirable to the dog, so it's normally safe to pull it away and refill the holes. Always make a grand show of refilling it so the dog cottons on to the fact that it's you making the bone tasty again. Hold the bone for the dog again. I continue this until the dog gets excited when I take the bone away. At this stage, the dog is never permitted to 'own' the bone—always hold it for him. At the end of a session, trade a treat for the bone and put the bone away so it's inaccessible to the dog.

Over a series of sessions, you can hold the bone closer and closer to the floor. Eventually, put the bone on the floor but hold it in place with your foot. Each time it's empty, reach down and take the bone away to refill it. This teaches the dog to relax while licking and chewing in close proximity to you and to welcome you reaching down to take the bone away. Once the dog is totally comfortable with this routine, introduce a new, more interesting chew toy, such as rawhide. Stick with 'single serving' chewies so the dog doesn't have leftovers to hide in the furniture.

Dogs who have learned to trust have no reason to defend their food and other treasures from people. Many puppies arrive in their new home prepared to fight for what they need, and it's imperative to teach them to trust you right from the start. This is accomplished by building their trust through exercises such as the ones described. Reacting with scolding, spanking, or removing the food more often than not makes the problem worse because you're confirming the dog's worst fear—that you are a competitor intent on stealing his treasures.

LEASH INDUCED AGGRESSION

Walking On the Wild Side

Exercising my dogs on the bike trails of New Jersey is very different from what I experienced in Toronto. The majority of dogs in Toronto are exercised in parks off the leash: chasing balls; wrestling with other dogs; or jogging with their owners. Dogs see other dogs, they stop and sniff, then carry on their way. The New Jersey dogs I've encountered tended to pull, bark and growl at other dogs.

Some owners scold me for having my dogs run free, while other express surprise that my dogs run alongside the bike without leashes. The local dogs are poorly socialized with other dogs, and many display what is called *leash-induced aggression*.

The alien experience

In her acclaimed book *The Culture Clash*, Jean Donaldson has us imagine that the earth has been taken over by aliens and we are kept as their pets. We are contained in cages, restrained by collars and leashes, and spoken to in a foreign tongue. From the time we leave our mothers, we are kept away from other people. We often see each other but rarely are we able to make contact. Just imagine how bizarre and frustrating that would be!

Dogs that display leash-induced aggression often started out as friendly sociable puppies. One plausible scenario goes like this: the pup becomes very excited when he sees other dogs on the street and pulls to say hello. The owner scolds the pup and pulls back on the leash or walks the other way. Each time this happens, the pup gets a little more frustrated. At some point, the frustration reaches a critical threshold and the pup needs an outlet to lessen his arousal. He tries barking, jumping or lunging on the leash. He feels a little better. These self-rewarding behaviours escalate and become conditioned to the sight of other dogs and to the feel of restraint from the leash. If the dog does get close to another dog, he can't subdue his emotions and he often comes on too strong or may even bite!

Contrast this with a puppy that has frequent contact with other puppies and dogs. He meets new dogs regularly and has plenty of opportunity to play. It's not such a big deal if this puppy gets pulled away from another dog on the street because, "Hey, it's just another dog." He knows that soon he'll be in the park where he can sniff butts and play to his heart's content.

Calling the dog's bluff

If caught early on, many of these leash-aggressive dogs come around with extensive socialization. I sometimes recommend daily sessions at an off-leash dog park. It's important, though, to take the dog off-leash *before* it meets the other dogs. If you are unsure how the dog will behave in this situation, use a basket muzzle to minimize risk for other dogs. Realize, however, that if the muzzled dog gets involved in an aggressive encounter, he is at a disadvantage and could be injured. I prefer to hand select a few dogs that are relatively unresponsive to aggressive threats and keep the potential aggressor on a long line to enable quick intervention if needed. Usually, the dog becomes a little more socially acceptable with each visit until he learns to interact and play with other dogs. Once he has the opportunity to meet and play with new dogs on a regular basis, his reaction to dogs on the street is usually attenuated because dogs are not such a novelty.

Street smarts

Leash-induced aggression is extremely easy to prevent by teaching a young puppy street smarts. In addition to allowing my puppy to socialize daily with other dogs, I condition him to expect treats from me when passing dogs and people on the street. Each time we see someone coming, I call him to me and allow him to nibble at a treat or tug on a toy as we walk by. Then, I put the treats or toy away until the next passerby. Pretty soon, the pup is looking at me every time someone approaches. Eventually my dog just ignores passing people and dogs but checks in with me just in case he might score a goodie!

The same procedure often works to eliminate well-established leash aggression. A dog that is highly food or toy motivated can be distracted by the owner, enabling the dog to get by without losing control. The original association of dogs passing by and feelings of frustration is replaced with a new association of dogs passing by and the anticipation of rewards. When the source of the rewards is the owner, the dog switches his attention from the other dog to the owner. Voila! No more uncontrollable aggression!

Some dogs need a little extra incentive to inhibit their obnoxious street behaviour. A client's Border Collie got so riled up that he didn't care about treats or toys when another dog was in view, even if he was on the opposite side of the street. We fitted him with a citronella anti-bark collar. The first time he barked at a dog, the collar activated and he got sprayed. He immediately stopped and looked around. Then he looked back at the dog and barked again. The collar sprayed again. The owner cued him to sit and rewarded him with a treat. After that, he was easy to distract with treats as the dog walked by. By the time four dogs had gone by, the Border Collie was trotting along beside the owner, eating snacks and completely ignoring the other dogs.

To be sure, not all dogs are this easy! I need to caution that it's imperative to make sure the citronella spray doesn't traumatize the dog and make things even worse. The use of punishment is sometimes warranted because it's necessary to find a means to inhibit the aggression so that acceptable behaviour can be encouraged and reinforced.

A vicious cycle

The biggest obstacle standing in the way of resolving leash-induced aggression is the leash. Sometimes just the feel of the leash snapping onto the collar is sufficient to get the dog aroused. When another dog is spotted, aggressive behaviour ensues. Without the leash, many dogs react in a friendly manner but, understandably, the owner is terrified to free the dog of the restraint for fear the dog would fight. And so, a vicious cycle is established. Breaking the cycle takes careful planning, experienced guidance and plenty of nerve!

THE THREE FACES
OF EEJ

Aggression Is a Complex Problem

As a behaviourist and trainer, I should have well-adjusted, perfectly behaved dogs, right? I suspect that's about as likely as the cobbler's son wearing shoes. I like to think that I learn something important from each of my dog's hang-ups, but my current dog, Eejit, is my biggest challenge yet. Eej is very bright, full of character, and the life of any party. He is extremely affectionate with people—large or small, old or young, pink or blue—doesn't matter to him as long as you're human. But he doesn't care for other dogs. He is, in fact, downright aggressive towards them.

I was inspired to write about my aggressive dog after attending an agility seminar a few weeks ago. This seminar was filled with experienced dog trainers and judges. I expected such a dog-savvy crowd to be knowledgeable about the complexities of aggression, but I was surprised by their naivety. In retrospect, I suppose what I observed was yet another example of the human desire for simple explanations: an aggressive dog is an aggressive dog, with no qualifications. Rarely is behaviour that simple.

A face only a mother could love

Eej has 'personal space issues' and he guards his stuff. If he's in an enclosed space, such as the car, or if he's in a training environment and another dog comes too close to him, he will lunge at the dog. He's worse if he's on a leash. He's especially volatile if we're playing or if he's really aroused from just running agility or flyball. He comes at the dog like a whirling dervish, taking his hapless victim by complete surprise. Fortunately, he's mostly noise and appears to have good bite inhibition—but every now and again he tears an ear or scrapes a face. And even without inflicting physical injury, he terrifies the dogs and their owners.

However, Eej has dog friends who can approach him under any circumstances, even take his bones or play with his toys, and he puts on a completely different face. He grovels and licks and whines with excitement. Seminar attendees shook their heads in confusion each time one of Eejit's buddies ran up to him because they saw such a different reaction from him.

After the first day of the seminar, several of us went for a walk along some trails in a nearby conservation area. Eejit was surrounded by six other dogs of various ages and sizes, including a few he had made nasty faces at earlier in the day. He trotted along with the group, sniffed the same trees and urinated on the same bushes. After a time, he chased and wrestled with one youngster. The next day at the seminar, the two new friends were playing Frisbee together in the adjacent field. But once back in the training facility, he would not tolerate this dog close to him. Several people were surprised at his Dr. Jeckyll and Mr. Hyde transformation, but Eej's personal space widens considerably when out in open spaces. It's as though if he feels he can escape, he's fine interacting with most any type of dog.

The face of an angel

Eej wasn't always a terror with other dogs. In fact, he was once great with dogs—submissive and playful. I'm afraid I took advantage of his skill at putting dogs at ease and used him to help dogs with aggression problems. He did his job well, but when I look at videotapes of those sessions, I recognize now that he was frightened of the dogs. His trust in dogs was further degraded at an agility trial, when his partner in a pairs class jumped him from behind while we were waiting for our turn to run. That was the first time he ever fought and I think he learned he was good at it.

Some dog enthusiasts don't realize that a dog can be aggressive to other dogs without ever displaying aggression to people. An agility competitor suggested that I ought to retire Eej from competition because he would surely attack a child. I wish she could see him work his magic with children. Eej occasionally works as a therapy dog and, in this context, he has the face of an angel. He sits with his tail wagging furiously and tries desperately to lick hands and faces. If the child is frightened of him, he lies down, shows his tummy, and doesn't move a muscle as the child summons the courage to touch him. He does his tricks, shares his toys, and gives up his bones. Eej has never met a person—young or old—that he doesn't like.

In need of a makeover

My attempts to 'fix' Eej have met with limited success, even though these methods have been effective with other problem dogs. The first few times I scolded him, assuming that if he understood I didn't want him behaving that way, he'd control himself. No chance. He behaves like someone 'gone postal'—it's like he's completely irrational and acts without thinking. If anything, he got worse when I scolded him, presumably because he was learning that I, too, lose my temper around other dogs.

I tried muzzling Eejit and taking him around plenty of friendly dogs so he could learn that no one is out to get him. Unfortunately, he was quite prepared to fight with the muzzle on, which wasn't fair to the friendly dogs, and I was risking him being injured too. Furthermore, he seems to feel trapped in the muzzle and becomes even more volatile. He was so stressed by these experiences that I couldn't bear to continue with this procedure. I was also running out of friends with dogs willing to serve as guinea pigs!

I've now settled on a promising combination of two techniques that I've discussed in previous essays: counter-conditioning and targeting. Whenever we are in show settings, Eej wears a head halter to give me increased control of his mouth, should he let fly. Each time a dog comes our way, we move a comfortable distance away and Eej gets special treats and attention from me. I want him to learn that avoiding dogs is a viable option, even when he's attached to me. If we cannot move, then I feed him continuously until the dog has passed by. This helps to keep his mind off the approaching dog *and* teaches him that the presence of other dogs is associated with good things for him.

Whenever I can recruit someone with a well-behaved dog to help me, I ask Eej to perform his targeting behaviour *to the other dog*. I first reward him for steps toward the dog, then for reaching out as though to sniff the dog from behind, then for approaching the dog from the side, and finally coming near the dog's face and sometimes even touching the dog. This is only feasible if the other dog is very attentive to his owner and doesn't try to turn and look at Eej. I'm hoping that Eejit comes to view greeting dogs as a learned behaviour that he does for treats, rather than as a stressful social behaviour.

Put on a happy face

Life with an aggressive dog is often fraught with worry. The owner must focus on managing situations to ensure everyone's safety while, at the same time, exploring the boundaries of the aggression so the dog's behaviour can be predicted reasonably well. When you're doing a good job of managing the dog, the lack of aggression sometimes lulls you into a false sense of security and you take unwarranted risks. Then, the dog ends up reacting and the cycle starts again.

It shouldn't come as a surprise to anyone that a dog can be nasty in one situation and friendly in another, even toward the same individual. Aggression is the result of specific environmental triggers. When these are identified, the objective is then to alter the dog's emotional response to the triggers. If the dog thinks "happy thoughts," the dog won't respond with aggression. Why just the other day, Eej met a new dog in his yard and he immediately put on his happy face and they were off and playing. With continued hard work and perseverance, I know I'll see more of that face.

2010 Update

I'm thrilled to report that Eejit, now 14½ years old, is the most incredible dog I've had the pleasure of sharing my life with. He retired from competitive agility just last year with many phenomenal runs and without ever harming a child (except maybe by licking one too determinedly). We worked hard on his dog aggression and, over the years, we made significant headway, although he can still erupt quite violently in very specific circumstances. But I know the triggers and happily, they are avoidable as long as I do my job. And that is my job as his partner. I hope he needs my protection for many years yet.

Scared Dog

Treating a Victim of Trauma

The young Flat Coated Retriever, Buddy, hides behind the owner's chair, peering out at me and growling. He runs out of the room, tail tucked, and appears in another doorway, watching me. If I move, a flurry of barking erupts. The owner recounts a story, his words laden with guilt, of how he tied Buddy to a garbage can outside a convenience store while he nipped in for a carton of milk. A rickety car backfired as it passed by and the frightened dog took off down the street, trailing the can behind him. A man selling Christmas trees recognized the danger to the dog and tackled Buddy as he ran by. Buddy was not impressed with the Good Samaritan—he bit the man's gloved hands and, when he couldn't escape, defecated in terror.

The repercussions

Virtually any dog would be traumatized by what Buddy went through. Some dogs can bounce back in a day or two but other dogs suffer long-term effects. Buddy's owner felt things were getting worse instead of better. Since that day, Buddy was increasingly reluctant to go for walks or car rides, reacted with extreme fear to sudden noises, and was terrified to meet anyone new. Guests could no longer come to the home because Buddy barks and growls for the duration of the visit.

Dogs with plenty of pleasant experiences on walks, meeting strangers, hearing traffic noises, and seeing the general bustle of city life, typically go through what is termed "spontaneous recovery." They might show fear for a few days but their former non-fearful behaviour recovers fairly easily. Dogs with a history of unpleasant experiences or young dogs placed in novel circumstances are more likely to display long-lasting fear after a traumatic event. Buddy was only six months old on that fateful day plus he was a nervous puppy. The owner reported that Buddy had always initially acted fearful with strangers but nothing like his current behaviour. He had been keen to go for walks but would shy away from loud traffic noises and vehicles moving close to the sidewalk.

What is fear?

Fear is a complex interplay of behavioural, emotional and physiological responses to certain stimuli. In the wild, fear is an adaptive behaviour that can serve to keep an animal safe from harm. Most animals, including humans, are hard-wired to respond effectively to the typical dangers encountered in their environments. My favorite example of this comes from a study with Rhesus monkeys. The researchers showed some monkeys a snake and other monkeys a flower. All the monkeys had'een raised in the laboratory and had no experience with either snakes or flowers and so none displayed fear. Immediately after being shown the item, however, the monkeys heard a loud, frightening noise. All the monkeys developed a strong fear of snakes but few showed any fear of flowers. This makes sense—snakes pose a real threat to the safety of most primates but flowers are unlikely to be hazardous!

This suggests there may be a genetic basis for the development of some fearful behaviour. Breeders can usually recount stories about progeny from a specific stud dog that react with fear to novelty. Researchers in the 1970's bred two strains of Pointers, one that exhibited extreme fear to noise, novelty, and people and one that rarely displayed fear. The abnormal dogs were quite resistant to attempts to eradicate their fears.

It is also well established that the early experience of an animal can also have a profound effect on the development of fear. Dogs with restricted experience of humans or novel environments from an early age show fear when exposed to them later. This describes Buddy, who was adopted from a breeder in a remote location at sixteen weeks of age. City life was a whole new experience to this sheltered country boy and he was convinced he didn't like it!

Turning Buddy around

Buddy needed to be helped quickly so that his phobias would not continue to escalate. Fearful behaviour is highly self-reinforcing because each time Buddy attempts to flee from a scary event, he further frightens himself. The first initiative of treatment is to avoid situations that prove too much for him to handle. For now, Buddy should not be forced to walk on city streets or meet new people.

The owner first worked on conditioning Buddy to be comfortable traveling in the car. He was fed in the parked car, he was cuddled in the car, and he was taken for very short rides to visit a friend with a playful dog. To minimize street noises, the car radio played a recording of home noises and Buddy was given a Kong stuffed with goodies to keep him occupied. Buddy also really enjoyed playing with the friend's dog. Once he looked forward to trips in the car, the owner was able to take Buddy to an off-leash park. Buddy began to make friends with the people associated with his new doggy playmates— friendships that were solidified through offerings of yummy treats. Then Buddy's owner began parking the car a block or so away from the park and Buddy was walked the rest of the way. This made walking relatively easy because Buddy knew how far he had to walk to get to the park. Each day, Buddy had to walk a bit further until, after several weeks, he was walking all the way from home.

Buddy was able to overcome his anxiety about guests in the home by first recruiting his new acquaintances at the park to come for visits. He already knew these people and associated them with treats. Each day a guest was scheduled to visit, Buddy was not given his regular meal. Instead, the bowl of food was placed outside the door for the guest to 'deliver' to Buddy on arrival. Lots of goodies and play for Buddy dominated these visits. Buddy began to look forward to visitors and, with experience, this anticipation transferred to entirely new people.

A happy ending

When I first met Buddy, his owner was extremely distraught. He had wanted a dog for years and the timing was finally right. He hoped for a companion that could go everywhere with him. He was a dedicated hiker and his goal for Buddy's first summer was to do the Bruce Trail. He was sure that he'd never accomplish his dream but he couldn't part with Buddy, no matter how unsuitable a companion Buddy appeared to be.

The happy news is that Buddy's dedicated owner worked very hard that winter to help Buddy overcome his fears. Despite a couple of setbacks and the need for a short-term course of an anti-anxiety medication, Buddy emerged as a more stable and confident dog. Best of all, the two had a wonderful hiking holiday together the following August.

GRRR!
DON'T TOUCH ME!

A Dog Who Can't Handle
Being Handled

The distraught caller identified herself as the owner of a top show dog—a male Yorkshire Terrier named Grady. The dog's handler had returned Grady because he was regularly being excused from the ring for growling at the judge. What was the owner to do? She had such great plans for this exceptional dog.

I went to meet Grady and learn more about him. He was well received in the ring, right from day one, and had been shown regularly for the past year. He was presented by several different handlers and hadn't lived at home since he was six months old. He saw his owner occasionally at shows. Now that he was home again, the owner reported that he seemed fine unless someone bent over him, reached for him, or put him on a table. Then he would growl, show his teeth and, in a few instances, even snap.

He seemed uninterested in me unless I approached him. Then he'd watch me warily—if I tried to reach for him, he'd growl and back away. When he was held on a grooming table, he became stiff. If I insisted on touching him, he growled until I moved away.

Grady was suffering from what I call touch sensitivity—a fear of being touched. He was particularly susceptible because *everyone* felt compelled to touch, poke and prod at him to determine whether he really was as good as he looked under all that luxurious hair. He was tired of it! Growling was an effective behaviour—it made people back off, which is exactly what he wanted.

Small breed susceptibility

Small breeds are more likely to develop touch sensitivity because people always want to pick them up. The syndrome starts when the dog is young—a cute toy breed puppy is like a magnet.

Years ago, I owned a friendly, well-socialized Yorkshire Terrier named Rael. I never thought twice about handing her over to anyone who wanted to hold her, until I took her to a college party. It was like a receiving line at a wedding. She was passed around the room from one set of hands to the next, until she finally had enough and snapped at someone. After that, Rael refused to be held by anyone with whom she didn't feel comfortable. For the remainder of her life, she barked and ran away from strangers.

Prevention and treatment

Preventing the development of touch sensitivity can be accomplished by ensuring that touching and holding are extremely positive experiences for the puppy. Teach him that rough and tumble play with people is fun. Get him used to being pushed and prodded, yanked and tugged. Have people hold the puppy and offer him special treats or play with his favorite toy. With a promising show prospect, have people examine the pup while you feed and praise him.

Treating an adult dog with touch sensitivity requires a more gradual and patient approach. For Grady, I recommended that everyone in the family make a point of *not* touching him for a few weeks. I wanted him to be able to relax and not dread interacting with people. Then, family and friends rewarded him with treats every time he approached them on his own.

Once he was hanging around people again, play was introduced. We started by inviting him to tug on his favourite toys. Occasionally someone would reach in to touch him—lightly at first, and then gradually with more intensity. Eventually, the toy was dragged over a low table onto which Grady was able to jump. Periodically, the game would cease and he'd be requested to stand in order to initiate the game again. This was often done on the table.

Over many weeks, we built up Grady's tolerance for all sorts of approaches and reaching movements, particularly when he was on the table. We wanted him to associate approach and touch with the positive feelings experienced during play. Each session was kept short because it would be easy to overwhelm him and make the problem worse.

The final, most difficult step required Grady to stand on the table while a stranger approached and examined him. It was necessary to repeat the sequence hundreds of times with people approaching to feed him or initiate play. This was done at home, in the local park, at obedience school, and at matches with cooperative judges.

The comeback

Grady's owner was motivated to get him back into the show ring, and she worked hard to reverse his attitude about being examined physically. Because of her dedication, Grady now thinks every judge is coming to play with him. His ears are up, his tail is wagging, and his attitude is back—he loves showing again!

MAKING FRIENDS

Targeting Teaches a Fearful Pup How to Meet Strangers

Like all five-month-old Golden Retriever puppies, Abbey was a people magnet! I watched from afar as children and adults in the park flocked around to meet the cute pup. Abbey, however, wanted none of it. She crouched behind her owner's feet, shying away from the outreached hands. A small boy offered a treat and she stretched tentatively to grab it. When the boy moved to touch her, she retreated to the end of her leash and froze in terror.

Abbey had lived with her breeder in a rural home until she was adopted by a young couple two weeks earlier. The new owners were understandably concerned about Abbey's fear, especially of children, as they were planning to adopt a baby within the next year.

Abbey's owners had borrowed the video *On Target!* by Gary Wilkes and were busily teaching Abbey to touch her nose to the end of a stick. The idea behind target training is that the animal learns to track and touch an object, usually a "target stick," which then permits the trainer to lure the animal into performing desired behaviours. Target training has become extremely popular among trainers in zoo settings for moving animals from one enclosure to another, positioning animals on weigh scales and focusing animals on a target while simple medical procedures are performed. Some trainers are now using target training to teach horses to load easily into trailers for transport.

Abbey was very motivated by food and seemed to enjoy the challenge of following and touching the stick. She lost herself so much in this activity that she didn't even notice when the owner held the stick in such a way that she had to approach me. She was even willing to touch the stick resting against my leg. Could targeting be used to help Abbey learn to enjoy interacting with people?

Making friends

Our first goal was to teach Abbey to approach strangers on cue. For this, we used the stick to 'point' to people. We recruited calm friends who would be good at following instructions, so Abbey wouldn't be too nervous around them. Initially the person just sat quietly, without looking at Abbey, while she moved closer and closer to the person in order to touch the stick for treats. Eventually, the stick was placed against the person's leg. She had no problem touching the stick like this, so the next step was to remove the stick just as Abbey's nose moved toward it, so that she would inadvertently touch the person's leg instead. Jackpot! Abbey got a delicious bit of steak for that. We continued until the stick was used to point to the person's leg and Abbey ran over and touched the leg for her treat. We cued the behaviour with the words, "Go make a friend."

Once Abbey was eagerly approaching and gently nosing numerous adults, the next step was to try the behaviour with children. Abbey's predominant behaviour was to run away when frightened. Because she had never been aggressive to anyone, we deemed it relatively safe to involve a dog savvy, ten year old boy. We did start, however, with the boy behind a baby gate as an extra precaution.

At first, Abbey was tentative about approaching the child but she seemed to recognize quite quickly that this was the same fun game as before. Within a few minutes, she was prancing up to the boy, now out from behind the gate, to touch his leg, once she was told to, "Go make a friend." Each time she did this, she eagerly turned back to look at her owner, as if to ask, "Did I earn a treat?"

A helping hand

Despite Abbey's new willingness to approach people, she would still retreat if anyone tried to touch her. This was the next obstacle to overcome. Her owners taught Abbey to target her nose on their hand, with the cue "Touch." She learned very quickly because of the similarity to touching the stick. To Abbey, an outstretched hand was now a signal to perform an approach behaviour for a treat. The owners made sure she was completely comfortable with their hands over her head, appearing from behind, and moving forcefully or un-expectedly.

Transferring the touch behaviour from their hands to the hands of strangers progressed quite well, but it became apparent that we needed one additional step. The people we recruited to help weren't content to just reach out and wait for Abbey to come to them. They wanted to stroke her and Abbey did not want to be touched. So we taught Abbey a new behaviour: she had to approach the hand, touch it with her nose, and then slither her body underneath it in order to get the treat. She looked a lot like a cat rubbing its body on a person. Abbey's owners shaped this in tiny steps until Abbey did the whole sequence reliably.

Persistence reaps rewards

It took several months for Abbey to accomplish the target training. The owners worked very hard teaching her the behaviours and then generalizing them to new people.

Transferring to children was especially problematic because children are less able to follow directions than adults and setbacks occurred when a child was too pushy for her. At first, Abbey had to be cued by her owners to approach people but now she happily trots up to just about anyone on the off-chance she might earn a treat.

Abbey has become much more comfortable in her interactions with people but she is still no social butterfly. Her timid nature prevents her from enjoying social contact for its own worth. Will she ever become a 'people-person'? Maybe; maybe not. This program worked for Abbey because we were able to remove the social essence of the greeting behaviour. Instead of trying to teach her to enjoy social greetings, we changed the nature of the greeting routine so that it was not social. Greeting people became a learned behaviour that she performed for her owners.

So the next time you find yourself in a Toronto park, keep an eye out for a beautiful, young Golden Retriever named Abbey. And don't be surprised if she gets you in her sights and comes running up to poke you with her nose. You've been targeted!

THE DOMINANT DOG

The Catch-all for Behaviour Problems

Ralph, a one year old Golden Retriever, is becoming a serious problem for his owner Sally. He steals things, such as Kleenex and shoes, and guards them. He growls and shows his teeth, and if Sally tries to reach for him or for the object, he bites her. Ralph charges out the door to go for his walks, and proceeds to pull Sally all the way to the park. He also barks at Sally for his dinner.

One interpretation of Ralph's behaviour is that he considers himself 'top dog,' and behaves obnoxiously in order to assert himself over Sally. Proponents of this 'dominance theory' explanation would probably advise Sally to refrain from allowing Ralph on the bed, to have him wait for her to proceed through doors first, to feed him only after she has finished her own dinner, and to require that he spend a good bit of time each day lying by her feet. These are indirect means of trying to reverse the status quo and establish Sally as the new 'alpha.' More direct approaches involve physical confrontations that often result in both dog and owner getting injured. But does the concept of dominance really help us understand and influence the relationship between a dog and his owner?

What is dominance theory?

The concept of dominance arose from studies of the social behaviour of chickens. A new flock of chickens will quickly form what is called a pecking order or linear hierarchy. Adult wolves confined together in an enclosure also form hierarchies, but they are far more convoluted than a simple pecking order. For example, Joe Wolf might be able to barge in ahead of Fred Wolf at a feeding site, but Fred can always displace Joe from his favorite resting spot. This is called a *context-specific* hierarchy because whichever wolf can pull rank depends upon the circumstances. Wolves also form alliances between family and friends. Sam might be subordinate to Joe when alone, but not when Al is present because Sam and Al are brothers. And recognize that this is a description of what happens with captive wolves. Wild wolves tend to live in families—a breeding pair and their offspring and so dominance hierarchies are usually moot. It's your age and role in the family that determines your access to things.

It is quite certain that dogs have evolved from wolves and, therefore, we expect similarities in their behaviour. However, there are some pretty major differences between dogs and wolves. For thousands of years, the dog has been selectively bred to show friendly behaviour characteristic of a subordinate or an immature wolf. A dog will routinely display submissive behaviours, such as wagging its tail, licking and rolling over onto its back. This suggests that domestication has had a major impact on dog social behaviour, and so it is extremely unlikely that what we observe in packs of captive wolves will map directly onto what we observe in households of dogs and people.

Studies of feral dogs also reveal a less than perfect match between the behaviours of dogs and wolves. Hierarchies in groups of feral dogs are poorly defined and quite unstable. Dogs move in and out of groups frequently and even travel alone for extended periods. Groups can be tolerant of unfamiliar dogs, but new members are often welcomed into the group. With this type of arrangement, a dominance hierarchy is not as useful as a simple rule-of-thumb for access to resources, say finders keepers.

Is Ralph a dominant dog?

Explaining Ralph's behaviour problems as resulting from Sally's failure to establish dominance over him is based on a *simplified* notion of dominance relationships. Would Ralph still be considered dominant if we analyze him in terms of a more complex and accurate view of *canid* social behaviour?

Ralph likes to guard his possessions. So do many subordinate dogs. It's true that dominant animals typically enjoy privileges, such as gaining access to food, resting places and mates. However, status may not be as important as ownership for dogs. Even an extremely submissive dog may vigorously defend a piece of food or bone that is within its 'ownership zone.' So, while a dominant animal may be able to access what food is available, it is often not able to take food *away* from a subordinate.

Ralph likes to lead the way, dragging Sally out the door and down the street to the park. While it's true that dominant animals are more likely to control group movements and dominant wolves lead hunts more often than subordinates, subordinates often become restless and attempt to start the group moving. Whether or not this is successful depends upon whether the dominant animals confer. And, after a successful hunt, if the dominant wolves have eaten their fill but the subordinate wolves are still hungry, they will embark on their own hunt.

Ralph tells Sally when it's time to eat. Subordinate animals also communicate how hungry they are. They certainly don't all lie around and politely wait for the dominant animals to finish their meal. Watch any nature show on social predators—there's tremendous chaos around a carcass. It's sometimes hard to believe anyone can get a decent meal!

According to this analysis, Ralph might be dominant or he might be subordinate to Sally. We can't tell from the information provided. Is there a better way to understand his problems?

It is always a good idea to start by examining the circumstances that led to the development of Ralph's bad behaviour. Sally says he was an active puppy, and she is a mature woman with a busy life. Ralph probably learned two important things during his first few weeks with Sally: 1) if he was tired and resting, Sally would ignore him and go about her business; and 2) if he wanted Sally's attention, a sure-fire way to get it was to grab a pair of shoes or knock over the garbage and run amok with a Kleenex. If Ralph gave the object to Sally, the game was over and she went back to doing other things, *but if he kept the object*, the game escalated into a chase or tug-of-war. Ralph learned that stealing was the way to initiate a game and keeping possession of the object was the way to prolong the game. Hence he became a resource guarder.

Ralph also learned that walks are *the* most exciting part of his day. Once they reach the park, Ralph is let loose to play with other dogs. From Ralph's perspective, the faster he gets to the park, the quicker the fun starts! Straightforward reward-based learning.

Lastly, when Ralph was a puppy, Sally thought it was cute when he whined at the cupboard where the cookies were kept. She couldn't resist that adorable face and always gave him something. Ralph didn't need to be a rocket scientist to learn that if he wanted to eat, go into the kitchen and bark! Operant conditioning reigns supreme.

With this additional information, techniques for changing Ralph's behaviour are revealed. Sally can teach Ralph appropriate ways to get her attention by making it difficult for him to steal things and easy for him to do other things that she can reinforce with positive attention and games. She can teach Ralph that the harder he pulls to get to the park, the longer it will take for him to get there. And she can teach Ralph that he will never again be fed for barking.

The steps reverse what Ralph already learned through Sally's unintended teaching. Maybe Ralph is dominant, and maybe he isn't. Or maybe it doesn't matter. In this case, applying dominance theory didn't lead to a clear path for changing his behaviour whereas an examination of his leaning history did. We understand so little about the intricacies of dog social behaviour that it seems the label of 'dominance' serves as a catch-all for a myriad of behaviour problems. If we use the label more judiciously, I think more dogs like Ralph will have a chance for rehabilitation.

I'm So Lonesome I Could Cry

Methods for Coping With Separation Anxiety

A young Welsh Springer Spaniel, Hogan, began trembling and panting as soon as his owner, Joan, picked up her briefcase and keys. By the time she stepped out and closed the door, Hogan was howling and racing back and forth between the front window and the door. Occasionally, he squatted and urinated.

Previously, Hogan had been surrendered to a breed-rescue group. His owners were divorcing and no one wanted custody of him. Joan had adopted Hogan two weeks ago. Already she'd received a complaint from the neighbors about the dog's howling. Understandably, she was not impressed with urine on her carpets and sofa, either. Reluctantly, she planned to return Hogan to the rescue organization.

Hogan, as a young adult being rehomed after a stable life with one family, was a prime candidate for developing separation anxiety. It appears that suffering any kind of loss makes dogs susceptible to the fear of being abandoned again.

Reacting to isolation is adaptive

Dogs are social creatures. When left to fend for themselves, feral dogs form loose groups and hang out together. Maybe a few moms and their offspring will join up for a few days; then some might go off with a cute male to investigate the local dump. It's not often you see a feral dog completely on its own. When a dog is alone and doesn't want to be, it barks or howls to find others.

The tendency to vocalize when isolated stems from puppy behaviour. If a puppy wanders off or in some way becomes separated from the litter, his natural response is to cry. Mom comes running to retrieve the lost puppy and bring him back to the den.

When a puppy arrives in his new home, he behaves the same way when isolated from his human family. Most puppies, however, eventually learn to accept that they will be left alone for periods of time.

When behaviour goes awry

A fearful reaction to being alone is sometimes manifested in adulthood. Some dogs just never learn to tolerate being left alone as puppies; others develop a fear of being left alone after a traumatic event or a change in the owner's schedule.

The anxiety associated with being left alone causes dogs to behave in various ways. Some vocalize, soil the house, chew things up or attempt to escape by digging and scratching at windows and doors. Others become subdued, seemingly depressed, and refuse to eat, play or do much of anything. Most dogs show a mixture of anxiety-related behaviours. Dogs typically get especially wrought-up within the first twenty to forty minutes after the owner leaves, which is when they tend to feel the greatest anxiety.

Be aware that a dog may also engage in many of these same activities if he's not anxious. Maybe he's bored and just enjoys ripping stuff up, maybe he likes to watch out windows and bark at passersby, or maybe he's not fully housetrained. A diagnosis of separation anxiety is warranted if the dog appears nervous and panicky; he engages in the problem behaviour only when the owner is absent and never when the owner is home, and the behaviour happens consistently every time the owner leaves. It can help to set up a video camera to spy on the dog and see if he is truly upset when he's alone.

Preventing separation anxiety

From the time the puppy first steps into his new home, the owner should begin teaching him that being alone is an okay experience. A Kong stuffed with something gooey and tasty, like peanut butter or cheese, or any of the plethora of food-stuffable toys now available are great tools for teaching a puppy to enjoy time spent alone. Give the puppy the toy and then leave, being sure to come back before the toy is empty. Remove the toy as soon as you return. Repeat this a few times and your puppy will be begging you to leave and not come back! Always begin with very short absences and gradually progress to longer and longer time periods.

Rehabilitating an anxious dog

An extremely anxious dog like Hogan may not benefit from 'Kong therapy' because he's too upset to eat. Joan reported that she tried giving Hogan a special treat prior to leaving and the treat would still be in the same spot hours later when she returned. Hogan would greet her enthusiastically and then dive for the treat!

Punishing Hogan when she returned to discover that her carpets were covered in urine definitely would not help, either. In fact, it would probably exacerbate the problem. Hogan is behaving this way because he's terribly anxious about being left alone. If he now worries about Joan coming home because of the punishment she metes out, he's liable to get even more uptight. Hogan is not able to control his behaviour any more than a person is able to stop his body trembling or his heart racing before giving a public speech, so it's really unfair to punish him for his misdeeds.

Confining Hogan in a crate or small room could also make him feel worse. Hogan, unable to move around to alleviate his anxiety, would probably do everything in his power to escape the crate. Anxious dogs frequently injure their paws and mouth attempting to break out of confinement.

A dog like Hogan can be rehabilitated by teaching him that it's tolerable, perhaps even okay, to be left alone. Joan accomplished this by exposing Hogan to extremely short absences to begin with and then gradually increasing the duration of her absence—but only as long as he remained relaxed. At first, Hogan would get upset when Joan simply walked near the front door. So Joan taught him to do a down-stay by the bedroom door. Joan began stepping behind the bedroom door and then popping back out to reward Hogan for staying. The bedroom was a good choice because Hogan had no 'baggage' associated with that door.

Once Hogan was able to stay while Joan disappeared behind the closed bedroom door for three minutes, the 'game' was then moved to the front door. At first, Joan and Hogan practiced very short stays without Joan venturing near the door. Instead, Joan rehearsed picking up her briefcase and keys while Hogan stayed put. Because Hogan didn't associate the new down-stay game with being left alone, he was fine. Joan started giving him a stuffed Kong to distract him as she prepared to introduce opening and closing the door.

Slowly but surely, Joan was able to increase the length of time she stayed outside, at first by one-minute increments, but eventually, as Hogan proved himself, by five-minute jumps. Joan made sure she did things like walk to the car, get in, and then come back inside. Or drive around the block. In due course, Hogan was waiting patiently for two to three hours. Then Joan resumed going to work—returning every few hours to say hello and provide a new food toy. With time, she was able to replace the frequent visits with a stopover by the neighbourhood dog walker. Joan breathed a huge sigh of relief, and Hogan was home to stay!

NOCTURNALLY
ACTIVE

Any Dog Can be Taught to Adapt to His Owner's Lifestyle

Does your dog become a party animal at night? Does he keep you awake—wanting to play, go outside, or just spend quality time together in the wee hours? I've met people who accept nocturnal activity as a necessary evil associated with owning a dog. I'm here to tell you it doesn't have to be that way.

Normal sleeping patterns

Dogs have evolved from predatory ancestors and so, by evolutionary design, are crepuscular (more active at dawn and dusk). This is common in predators because prey species are more abundant—although more difficult to see—at dawn and dusk.

Two Australian researchers, Ken Johnson and Graham Adams, conducted a number of studies to determine the normal sleep patterns of dogs. They compared dogs living in pet homes with dogs that can determine their own schedules, such as those that range freely or are loose on a property. If a dog is not influenced by the presence of people, he typically spends some of the night sleeping and some of it lying still but mentally alert. Interspersed are short periods of intense activity, such as chewing, playing or eliminating.

Dogs that live in a home tend to spend more time sleeping at night than dogs left to their own devices. However, they still show the characteristic sleep-wake cycles, usually spending roughly sixteen minutes asleep for every five minutes awake. About half the night, the dog will be in slow wave sleep and can easily be aroused. The rest of the time, the dog will be in active REM sleep. This is when his limbs twitch or he may vocalize. Presumably, this is when dogs dream.

Nocturnal activity in puppies

Given the cyclical nature of the dog's sleep-wake pattern, it's not surprising that a young puppy often wakes during the night. Because of his immature plumbing, the puppy will need to eliminate and so he cries to be released from the crate. It's perfectly appropriate for you to wake up, take the puppy to his toileting area, reinforce him for alerting you to his need, return him to the crate, and go back to sleep. This can become a significant problem, though, if the puppy learns that waking up and crying is an effective means for obtaining the owner's undivided attention.

This places the owner in a real bind. If you ignore the puppy, and he really needs to 'go,' he may eliminate in his crate which means you have a screaming puppy and a major mess to contend with. However, if you attend to the puppy, you risk spending the rest of the dog's life waking up each night!

My strategy for avoiding that latter problem is to behave quite differently during the night than I do during the day. I expect I'm never very friendly in the middle of the night anyway but, when the puppy is young and can't hold his urine for any length of time, I try to be fairly neutral. Once the puppy has demonstrated the ability to wait to urinate, I become quite unpleasant at night. At first, I ignore the puppy for a few minutes. If the whining continues, I pick the puppy up (all the while grumbling uncontrollably), take him to this toilet area, stand and grumble some more, and plunk him back in his crate as soon as he's done. I realize this is absolutely the worst thing you can do for encouraging house-training but, at night, my priority is to teach the puppy to keep quiet unless disaster is about to strike. This procedure seems to work—all my dogs have learned to sleep through the night *unless* they have a diarrhea emergency.

Nocturnal activity in adults

Dogs that are active during the night are usually dogs that are alone for extended periods of time during the day. They haven't received sufficient exercise and attention and have discovered a surefire way to obtain it at night! Most respond well to a rigorous bout of exercise first thing in the morning before the owner leaves for work, combined with plenty of exercise, training and attention during the evening. In some resistant cases, melatonin can help the adult dog adapt to the family's schedule of sleeping through the night. Although melatonin is a natural substance produced by the body when preparing to sleep, be sure to consult with your veterinarian before administering over-the-counter supplements like this one.

Nocturnal activity in the elderly

Aging dogs often develop a pattern of waking and wandering about the house during the night, sometimes whining or barking. In some cases, they appear quite panicked. While we don't completely understand why this occurs, one thought is that elderly dogs simply wake up periodically, as all dogs do, and then panic and start moving around—either because they don't recognize their surroundings or don't understand why they're alone. Elderly dogs showing this type of nocturnal behaviour sometimes respond to treatment with selegiline (L-deprenyl), a monoamine oxidase inhibitor (Type B) that is used to treat cognitive dysfunction in aging dogs. Other old dogs respond better to anti-anxiety medications.

Researchers have speculated that another possibility is that the dog's circadian rhythm is disrupted as a result of age-related damage to the pituitary gland. For these dogs, melatonin may help reset the sleep-wake cycle back to normal.

No more sleepless nights

Invariably, dogs are expected to adapt their lives to the wishes of their human counterparts. Without our interference, the dogs would naturally sleep a bit, run around a bit, and hang out a lot, not doing much of anything. They'd do this day AND night. However, by ensuring the dog doesn't enjoy human companionship at night and by providing him with adequate exercise and mental stimulation during the day, any dog can easily adapt to the diurnal lifestyle of his people. He'll sleep or remain quiet through the night, waking up with the alarm just like the rest of us. I only wish I could wake up in the morning with the same enthusiasm as my dogs!

WHEN LIGHTNING STRIKES

Can Fear of Thunder Be Cured?

Many people are thrilled to watch the occasional rainstorm, accompanied by impressive lightening flashes, booming thunder, and torrential rains. Not so the average dog owner—thunderstorms can be traumatic experiences for many noise-sensitive dogs.

Freda, a female Belgian Sheepdog, developed a fear of thunder at about fourteen months of age. During a storm, she would pace through the house, panting, and trembling. At the height of the storm, she'd dig frantically at the drain of the bathtub. Attempts to restrain her were futile—she would whine, struggle, and become even more distraught. Then one day there was a bad thunderstorm while Freda's owners were at work. They came home to a frightened mess of a dog, lying in a large pool of saliva, hiding behind the toilet. Thereafter, Freda was reactive to a large variety of sounds, including the noises generated by the tenant in the basement. If the tenant spoke on the telephone, coughed or sneezed, Freda would jump up, tail tucked and ears back, and begin pacing and panting. Other household sounds, such as the toilet flushing or the dishwasher running, triggered the same response. Freda was so desperate that she even tried blocking the owner from leaving each morning. Freda didn't appreciate being pushed out of the way and eventually bit her owner's arm. The poor dog was perpetually terrified in her own home.

The development of thunder phobia

My Border Collie developed a fear of thunder at just over one year of age, which is a common age of onset for noise phobias. He would startle at the sound of thunder and run to hide under the bed. He was inconsolable. He quickly learned the association between a cloudy sky and thunder and was often reluctant to go outside on dreary days. Surprisingly, his fear dissipated with age. Now at 10 years, he shows little reaction at all to thunder unless it is a very loud clap (and yes, his hearing is still excellent!). This is unusual, as most dogs get worse with age. It is thought this worsening might be due to neural degeneration that weakens the dog's ability to cope with stress.

Researchers tend to suspect that thunder-phobic responses in dogs are pretty hard-wired. Humans with panic disorder have, at times, abnormally high levels of norepinephrine excreting from an area of the brain called the *locus ceruleus*. Norepinephrine is the chemical normally released when we experience fright. These people have brains that are sometimes in a state of fright for no apparent reason. We don't yet know if the same is true of dogs with noise phobia. It has also been suggested that thunder-phobic dogs may have more sensitive hearing than non-reactive dogs.

Some thunder phobias can be traced back to a traumatic precipitating event but, unlike most learned fears, a phobia of thunder can be established after only one such exposure. In almost all cases, these animals do not become accustomed to storms with repeated exposures. Often they expand their fear to similar-sounding stimuli, such as firecrackers and gunshots. In Freda's case, she generalized to a wide variety of household sounds.

Can thunder phobia be cured?

Noise phobia may be treated through the use of recordings of thunder to which your dog reacts and you can control the volume. The dog is taught to stop being afraid through desensitization and counter-conditioning. The dog is exposed to the sound of thunder, beginning at a level so low that it does not elicit a fearful response, while concurrently associating the sound with pleasant things, such as relaxing massage and food pacifiers. I recommend that owners identify a place where the dog feels secure—for Freda, it was in a dark closet off the master bedroom. Once a day, her owner made Freda comfortable in her closet, offered her a Kong stuffed with peanut butter and special treats, and sat down to give her a gentle massage. To start, the volume of the recorded storm was set extremely low, but gradually, over several sessions, it was increased to an audible level. Occasionally Freda did show concern, particularly if there was a loud clap of thunder on the CD. When this occurred the owner exclaimed, "Oh what was that?" and gave Freda a delicious piece of steak or chicken—treats Freda found irresistible. If she didn't relax after a few minutes at the increased level, the owner backed up to a previous level and stayed there a bit longer before trying to progress again.

Each session lasted forty-five to sixty minutes, because long sessions have been shown to be more effective for this type of fear. Over the course of several weeks, Freda was able to relax through louder and louder recorded storms. The owner was careful to change the recording every few sessions and to move the loudspeakers around the house.

One important component of this technique is that during treatment, the dog must not experience a full-blown fear reaction to the real thing. In other words, you can't treat thunder phobia during thunderstorm season! If you try, your dog will likely experience a real storm during the treatment and this will set you back to square one.

What if your dog is not fooled by recordings?
Unfortunately, many thunder-phobic dogs learn the associated stimuli that signal an oncoming storm, such as clouds in the sky, atmospheric changes, rain, and lightning. These dogs are more difficult to fool with recordings. Believe it or not, my Border Collie would go to the window and, if the sky was clear, he wouldn't react to the storm on my CD! Some behaviourists have experienced success by adding extra features, such as strobe lights to simulate lightning and water sprinklers against the windows to simulate rain.

Making the transition to the real thing

Making the transition to real storms is where most treatment programs run aground. Success is maximized by making the real event as much like the simulated-storm environment you've created as possible. This is best done by paying close attention to the weather forecast so you and your dog are ready. Well before the first storm hit, Freda's owner made her comfortable in her closet and recreated the relaxation session as before. The volume of the recorded storm was as loud as Freda could tolerate. As the real storm built up steam, Freda's owner was ready with the extra special steak bits. For each clap of real thunder, Freda got the especially wonderful treats. As far as Freda was concerned, this was just another session with a slightly different recording. With subsequent storms, the owner gradually lowered the volume of the recording so that the real storm became the predominant sound. Eventually, Freda was fine during a storm, provided she could escape to her safe place.

Can drugs help?

The use of drugs is warranted if your dog does not respond to artificial storms and so is less likely to benefit from desensitization and counter-conditioning sessions. Some dogs will also progress through the treatment sessions more quickly or more successfully if given anti-anxiety medication. Beneficial results have been reported for a variety of anti-anxiety medications, such as those used with phobic human patients. Dogs that do not respond to treatment and risk injuring themselves during storms often need heavy sedation to manage them safely. Be sure to use drugs that are anxiolytic. The medication Acepromazine (Atravet) is sometimes recommended for thunder-phobic dogs, but its anti-anxiety effects are questionable and it can actually increase sensitivity to noises. However, Atravet can be used in combination with other anti-anxiety medication to help treat noise phobias.

Freda's future

In addition to treating Freda's fear of thunder, we also had to address her reaction to the tenant's noises. This was accomplished using the same procedure, although we didn't have Freda in the closet because the eventual goal was for her to function normally in the presence of

these everyday household sounds. It was much more difficult to minimize her exposure to the real sounds during treatment. The owner
played loud music to mask the tenant's sounds and, at particularly
noisy times, Freda was encouraged to spend time in the backyard.
The good news was that as Freda became more comfortable in her
home, her aggression toward the owner dissipated. The owner was
thrilled because, before calling me, she was torn as to whether she
needed to find a new home for her dog or find a new house with no
tenant so the dog wouldn't be afraid!

MEAN CUISINE

Curbing Your Dog's Distasteful Eating Habits With Aversion Conditioning

Dogs can be odd creatures when it comes to their eating habits. Some dogs delight in consuming all sorts of unusual items, such as shoes, Kleenex, rocks, dead animals and, horror of horrors, feces and vomit.

Do dogs taste what they eat?

Yes, believe it or not, dogs do have well-developed taste buds for sweet and bitter, nucleotides (meaty tastes), furanol (fruity tastes), and acids. So we know they taste what they eat. Why, then, do some dogs develop appetites for such abhorrent things? The idea that these dogs are lacking in some necessary nutrient or mineral is a popular one, but it has never received scientific confirmation.

It's important to realize that some totally disgusting items are actually perfectly appropriate sources of food for a dog. Most *canid* species will happily scavenge a morsel of road kill—evolutionary speaking, their digestive systems are set up to handle putrid flesh. Some types of feces and regurgitated matter have digestible constituents that dogs can use. Deer and rabbits often eat their own feces as a means to further break down the vegetative matter and dogs can also benefit from those nutrients. Eating puppy feces is an adaptive behaviour pattern for lactating bitches—licking the puppy's anogenital region stimulates defecation and the dam ingests the fecal matter to keep the nest clean.

There is no doubt, however, that some dogs acquire a taste for their own or other dogs' feces, or the contents of the resident cat's litterbox (eating poop is called coprophagy). Some dogs habitually consume inedible things, and often the veterinarian ends up fishing stuff out of their intestines (this is called pica). No one knows why these tendencies develop in a small percentage of dogs.

Discouraging peculiar cravings

If you're the unfortunate owner of a dog with questionable gastronomic habits, such as poop eating, you've probably been counseled to prevent the dog from gaining access to feces by removing the dog or the feces. If you prefer to teach the dog *not to eat* poop, associating the act of eating it with a nasty consequence is the best recommendation. One option is to adulterate feces with hot or bitter tastes before the dog gains access to it. A second option is to add a substance to the dog's food that affects the taste of the poop before it comes out the other end.

Occasionally, the owner is advised to punish the undesirable eating behaviour with the use of a nasty sound, a sudden spray of water, a frightening movement like a triggered mousetrap placed next to the feces, or a painful or startling shock. All of these options have worked in certain circumstances.

Taste aversion learning

A well-established scientific procedure for teaching animals to avoid eating certain foods is called taste aversion conditioning. Almost all animals—and people too—are highly prepared to learn to avoid any food that is associated with illness. My first experience with taste aversion occurred years ago after eating at a Mexican restaurant. Unfortunately, the food was bad and I became ill. Now, even the mention of Mexican food makes me feel nauseous. I became conditioned to associate the taste of the food with the illness that I felt afterwards.

Anyone who has undergone chemotherapy will tell you a similar story. Chemotherapy causes nausea, but the person often becomes conditioned to dislike the food that's been eaten prior to the onset of the illness. This occurs even though the person *knows* that the illness was caused by the chemotherapy and not the food.

Taste aversion conditioning has been used with considerable success to teach wild predators, such as wolves, coyotes, and mountain lions, not to kill and eat livestock. Sheep-meat baits, containing capsules of lithium chloride (a salt that induces illness about 20 minutes after ingestion), are scattered about in the predator's habitat. The animals eats the bait, becomes ill and, later, shows an intense revulsion to the smell of live sheep. Unfortunately, things can go awry because some animals still kill the sheep before turning away in disgust. However, when it works, even a very hungry wolf will pass by a pasture full of sheep without feeling tempted.

What approach works best?

A scientist named Carl Gustavson compared the success of a variety of techniques for teaching an animal not to eat a favorite 'food.' He offered rats Oreo cookies, their most preferred food in the world. He compared five different procedures for putting the rats off Oreos—a shock, the smell of ammonia, hot mustard, quinine (a very bitter flavor), or taste aversion conditioning with lithium chloride. Gustavson found that only taste aversion conditioning completely destroyed the rats' passion for Oreos. Rats that were shocked showed some hesitation when next offered a cookie but, in the end, they succumbed to their desire. The nasty repellents—the ammonia, hot mustard, and quinine—had virtually no effect on the willingness of rats to eat Oreos.

Taste aversion conditioning has been used to teach dogs not to eat a variety of things, including chickens, specific fabrics, dirt, plants and feces. The learning occurs rapidly—often after only one illness— and can endure for the entire life of the dog. I should mention that lithium chloride is a very safe substance—a dog would have to eat an entire mountain of lithium chloride to suffer any significant damage.

What about the dog that eats a whole cake and vomits shortly thereafter? Why does this dog fail to show a learned aversion to cake? Dogs regurgitate for a variety of reasons and often dogs do not experience illness when they vomit. When they consume lithium chloride, *they feel sick*. They feel miserable and the effect lasts for a good hour or two.

Taste aversion conditioning is a bit messy because lithium chloride is difficult to work with. You have to hide it in the forbidden food, which can be rather revolting if you're working with feces. Far more compelling, though, is that taste aversion conditioning could save the life of a dog determined to eat things that can get stuck in his digestive tract. Be sure to consult with your veterinarian and a certified animal behaviourist or veterinary behaviourist before trying this at home.

Bizarre Behaviours

The Rare Compulsive Disorder

The chubby little Jack Russell Terrier, Buddy, began circling as soon as I entered the home. He circled backwards, grabbing at his front paw on each step. Looking closer, I saw that a toe was missing on the paw and the adjacent toe was red and raw. This poor dog was mutilating his own foot!

Buddy's owner, a recent widow, explained that Buddy had been a perfectly normal dog and the constant companion of her husband until his death. Shortly thereafter, she noticed Buddy licking at his front paw, but didn't give it another thought until he began the repetitive circling as well. She then noticed a lesion on his toe. A trip to the vet ruled out organic causes for the behaviour and a diagnosis of compulsive disorder was rendered. Buddy's toe was amputated in the hope that he would stop. To the owner's dismay, Buddy started on the adjacent toe.

What is compulsive disorder?

Compulsive disorder is diagnosed whenever an animal engages in repetitive, stereotypic behaviour that interferes with the animal's normal functioning. The behaviour serves no obvious purpose and can sometimes, as in Buddy's case, cause harm to the animal.

Dogs display many different forms of compulsions, such as spinning, pacing, tail chasing, snapping at the air, and excessive licking. Some breeds are predisposed to particular compulsive disorders. For instance, Doberman Pinchers, Golden Retrievers and Labrador Retrievers are prone to excessive licking (also known as acral lick dermatitis or lick granuloma). Bull Terriers are known for spinning and for the peculiar behaviour of freezing in one position, often with the dog's head stuck in a closet. German Shepherd dogs are vulnerable to tail chasing compulsions, sometimes removing all the hair or even mutilating the end of the tail. Some dogs will spend almost all their waking hours engaging in the repetitive behaviour, to the point of losing weight, suffering from exhaustion, and causing physical injury. Other dogs will engage in the behaviour only in response to certain triggers, such as excitement or frustration.

Why do some dogs develop compulsions?

It's generally believed that compulsive disorders are triggered initially by stress or conflict. In Buddy's case, it was the loss of his best friend. The repetitive behaviour serves to reduce the animal's stress, arousal level, or awareness of the situation, much the same as thumb sucking relaxes human children. Dogs that are at high risk for compulsive disorder are:

- Habitually tied up or confined and forced to live in close quarters

- In social conflict (such as experiencing a long separation from a companion or suffering frequent aggression from others in the group)

- Lacking opportunities for normal species-typical behaviour (such as when completely isolated from people and dogs)

- In a state of motivational conflict (for instance, a dog that needs to go into the yard to eliminate but is afraid to enter the yard because of a past frightening experience there)

- Unable to control their environment (for instance, a dog that is abused or punished randomly and unpredictably).

Dogs suffering from head injuries, bacterial and viral infections, or epilepsy also sometimes engage in compulsive behaviours but these are believed to develop differently.

The prevalence of compulsive disorder in dogs is unknown. The problem is documented in virtually all domesticated species, wild animals in confinement, and humans. Approximately two to three percent of people suffer from compulsive disorders (such as repeated hand washing, checking and rechecking that doors are locked, hoarding animals, etc.).

Similarly, two percent of all Thoroughbred horses show behaviours such as repetitive weaving, pawing and pacing. Some horses develop a behaviour called cribbing, in which they grasp a board or trough with their front incisors and gulp large amounts of air. Cribbing horses can wear their teeth down to nubs.

Research has revealed that although conflict and stress may initially trigger a compulsion, the behaviour often takes on a life of its own, even when triggering stimuli are absent, because of endorphin release in the brain. As the behaviour becomes established, animals and people experience a 'high' from it and they become addicted, much the same as an addict develops into a substance abuser.

Do all dogs with obsessions have compulsive disorder?

Fortunately, no! Most people who live with intense herding or terrier breeds are well accustomed to dog obsessions. My own Eejit, a Border Collie/Terrier cross, is a great example. He is obsessed with celestial objects—he will run and bark at the moon for hours on end. He especially likes it when it's visible during the day. He likes the sun too, especially if it's partially obscured behind some clouds. However, it would not be considered a compulsive disorder because he is easily diverted to a different activity and will do this crazy moon behaviour only if there's nothing else happening. I also do not allow him to go on for more than a few minutes at a time because I fear it could become a compulsion if he began to get off on the endorphin release.

Can compulsive disorder be cured?

Treating compulsive disorder is a real challenge because you are battling brain chemistry reinforcement. The standard approach involves a combination of behaviour modification and medication. If possible, all stimuli that trigger the behaviour are to be avoided or counter-conditioned. Owners need to be very aware of their own behaviour and resist inadvertently reinforcing the dog with attention. The anti-anxiety drug Clomipramine (Clomicalm), and others like it, can be helpful because it increases the level of serotonin in the brain. Finally, drastic increases in mental and physical stimulation can help. I can pinpoint exactly when Eejit's reaction to the moon started: we were on a long road trip and I was not exercising him as much as I should. If I had provided a more stimulating environment for him in the vehicle or had exercised him sufficiently en route, he might never have noticed that big 'eye' in the sky!

Buddy's condition was improved through a combination of medication and behaviour modification. He now licks at his foot occasionally, but is easily interrupted with by reminders to stop. His toe has healed and he's becoming very attached to the missus, who cherishes Buddy's company because he was such a devoted friend to her husband.

DOG TIRED

Behaviour Problems Can Be Avoided With Physical and Mental Exercise

Just think of the incredible diversity within the canine species: the Border Terrier can take on the toughest of vermin foes; the Dalmatian can run for miles next to a horse-drawn carriage; the Labrador can swim in freezing cold water; the Siberian Husky can pull a sled for hundreds of miles; the Border Collie can move sheep for hours on end. Many of the breeds with which we share our lives are animals that were selected for athleticism and intense mental concentration.

Contrast these images with the average urban dog's reality—wake up after eight hours of sleep, spend a bit of time in the backyard, eat, sleep for another eight hours, go for a thirty-minute walk around the neighborhood, eat, curl up on the couch and nap, go to bed again. Does urban life impact on the physical and mental well-being of dogs? You bet it does!

Most owners have only a vague notion of the original purpose of their dog's breed and even less of an idea how much exercise their dog requires. Few city dogs are mentally stimulated and physically challenged in ways that even remotely resemble the activities for which they were bred. Inactive bodies and minds are fertile grounds for the development of behavioural problems.

Looking for trouble

What's a bored dog to do? Look for trouble, that's what! Any dog of an energetic breed will discover some way to amuse himself and, more often than not, the owner will not like what the dog finds. I've seen a Sheltie that constantly herds caged gerbils, a Jack Russell that is obsessed with alarm clocks, and a Brittany that spends the entire day standing on the back of the sofa barking at everyone that passes by on the busy street. If a dog like this is provided with vigorous, healthy exercise twice a day, much of the obnoxious behaviour will 'magically' disappear.

Some dogs simply wait until left alone to find outlets for their energy. A dog that is extremely well behaved when the owner is home can become quite the party animal with the house to himself. Dogs often learn *exactly* what you teach them. They learn not to chew the furniture, get into the garbage and trail the toilet paper from room to room *when you are home*, because *you* deliver the unpleasant consequences. When you're not home, these activities are fair game.

Guarding against aggression

Some city dogs are taken to the park each day to hang out in large play groups with a mix of familiar and unfamiliar dogs. The dogs exercise through rough-and-tumble play and chase games. The owner's job is to drink coffee and discuss world events with other owners. A lot of dogs are fine with this arrangement, and it's an excellent form of exercise. However, too much of a good thing can be problematic. Hanging around in large play groups can foster aggression problems. Fights are likely to occur simply because of the density of animals in a small area. Squabbles happen when the play gets too rough or there is a dispute over ownership of a toy or the treats inside a human's pocket. Conflicts don't have to be numerous for a dog to start anticipating negative experiences in the play group. And a dog that is expecting a fight can over-react to the slightest threat and then the cycle of aggression begins.

It doesn't necessarily pay to avoid play groups either. Many dogs are exercised by walking on a leash next to their human. A leashed walk can be a good opportunity for practicing obedience but isn't real exercise for the average dog. Unless you are a speed walker, a stroll isn't long enough or strenuous enough to physically challenge a terrestrial quadruped like the dog.

The mental stimulation afforded by a walk is reasonably good, provided you vary the route so your dog is constantly processing novel sights, sounds and smells. The major liability with walking a dog on a leash is that he is frequently exposed to people and dogs. If your dog is friendly, he will keep trying to greet everyone and you, embarrassed by your dog's uninvited overtures, will keep pulling him away. Many dogs become frustrated. Almost inevitably, frustration leads to aggression. Your once friendly dog is still pulling and lunging towards people and/or dogs but his mission is no longer a sociable one.

Pay to play?

Dogs of busy owners often wave good-bye each morning, then snooze until the professional walker arrives for the daily exercise session. Is it a good idea to have your dog exercised by someone else? Not if you can do it yourself. Think of the advantages: fresh air to clean your head; exercise to revive your body; and, best of all, your dog will think you are the greatest! It saddens me to see a dog that adores the walker but barely acknowledges the owner. The dog isn't being disloyal or fickle—the walker simply signifies the highlight of the day for the dog. Strengthening the bond between you and your dog by being involved in the activities he loves is absolutely the best benefit of a daily exercise program.

Planning your dog's exercise

Two good outings, one in the morning and one in the evening, that combine some play time with other dogs, play with toys, and some energetic hiking or running is ideal for most dogs. Some dogs need more exercise than this and some require less. The best way to know if you are exercising your dog adequately is to examine his behaviour. Is he calm and quiet during the day? Does he sack out for a few hours after his regular run?

Variety also helps to stimulate the mind and the body. Attending weekly classes in agility, flyball, or other physically demanding sports adds spice to your dog's life.

Always consult with your veterinarian to make sure your dog can embark on a rigorous exercise program. Established couch potatoes will need to progress gradually. Young dogs should not be exercised strenuously until their growth plates have closed.

Excellent behaviour modification

Humans have genetically selected dogs to be phenomenal athletes with minds capable of fierce concentration. Now we ask them to live in urban spaces where their *raison d'être* is no longer. The more exercise you can provide your dog, the better he will behave. He'll be well socialized, used to all sorts of sights and sounds, view you as his special companion, and, best of all, he'll be dog tired!

Exercise is an excellent treatment for many behaviour problems because a tired dog is usually a good dog.

A Sound Mind in a Sound Body

Objectionable Behaviour Could Be Caused by an Underlying Physical Problem

Abbey the Boxer trembled and panted in the clinic waiting room. Her owner related to the receptionist how Abbey's separation anxiety had escalated dramatically in the past few weeks. While she had always barked and chewed things when left alone, she was now become very distressed during the night and sometimes even when the family moved to a different room. Instead of going with them, she whined and trembled, appearing reluctant to pass through the doorway. Just that morning she refused to come back into the house after going for her morning walk. Is this a case of separation distress, generalizing to a more widespread anxious state, or could there be another explanation?

Behaviour is a reflection of many influences: genetics; temperament; learning history; current environment; and physical health. Diagnosing a specific behavioural problem requires that organic conditions be ruled out first. Sadly, it turned out that Abbey's bizarre behavioural changes were due to a late-stage intracranial neoplasm—a brain tumor.

Brain and nervous system disorders

Brain tumors are more common in the dog than in other domesticated animals. Affected dogs tend to be at least five years of age when diagnosed. The behavioural changes associated with intracranial neoplasms depend upon the location and character of the tumor and can include aggression, apathy, excitability, seizures and disorientation.

Seizure disorders are often first presented as behavioural problems. Psychomotor seizures, which result from an abnormality of the limbic system, can lead to aggression or certain stereotypic behaviours such as hallucinatory fly-snapping and flank-biting.

Some behaviourists suggest that select cases of purported 'rage-syndrome' or idiopathic aggression (attacks that are apparently random and unprovoked) may also be the result of psychomotor seizure activity. While it's often difficult to definitively diagnose psychomotor epilepsy, the accepted criteria include: a) behaviour that is not congruent with the dog's history; b) accompanying clinical signs, including seizures or abnormal brain wave activity; and c) problem behaviour that can be elicited with epileptogenic drugs (medication that makes a seizure more likely) and inhibited by the use of antiepileptogenic drugs (medication to lessen seizure activity).

The issue of abnormalities in neurochemistry and, in particular, serotonergic dysfunction has received a great deal of attention. It's been established that, in humans, serotonin modulates aggression through the inhibition of impulsive behaviour. Convicted murderers and arsonists tend to have low levels of serotonin in their cerebral spinal fluid. The findings in dogs, however, are not definitive. One study revealed that serotonin levels in the cerebral spinal fluid were lower in dogs that displayed dominance-motivated aggression than in non-aggressive laboratory dogs.

Despite such findings, the effectiveness of serotonin-targeted medications—serotonin reuptake inhibitors such as Prozac, Paxil, and Zoloft—for reducing aggressive behaviour problems has been disappointing. While SSRIs may help in select cases, they are certainly far from a cure-all.

Metabolic disease

Dogs with a deficiency (hypo) or an excess (hyper) of thyroid hormone are occasionally presented for aggression problems. Aggression has also been reported as a problem for both hypo and hyper thyroid people, although it is much more common with hyperthyroidism.

A link between aggression and thyroid disease in dogs has not been clearly established and is a hotly debated topic. If it does occur, it tends to be in younger dogs in the early stages of thyroiditis.

It is accepted that hypothyroidism usually causes decreased activity and mental dullness in dogs, while hyperthyroidism can lead to nervousness, hyperactivity, and excessive drinking. While hyperthyroidism is rare in dogs, hypothyroidism is quite common. It's the most frequently diagnosed endocrine disease that dogs suffer from.

Aging problems

Elderly dogs may show behavioural changes attributable to canine cognitive dysfunction (senile dementia). Aging dogs can exhibit decreased responsiveness or attentiveness, reduced social affiliation, disorientation, and a breakdown in house training. Post-mortem studies of the brains of affected dogs show neuropathology similar to that seen in humans suffering from Alzheimer's disease.

Physical disease in older dogs, such as loss of hearing, loss of vision, and arthritis, can lead to irritability and, sometimes, aggression. Of course, these effects are not necessarily limited to old dogs—young dogs suffering from perceptual deficits or skeletal problems, such as hip dysplasia, may also be prone to testiness and aggression problems.

Elimination problems

House training problems in dogs often have an organic basis. Inflammatory diseases, such as cystitis, urethritis, irritable bowel syndrome and colitis can lead to urination or defecation accidents in the house. Unfortunately, the house soiling may persist even after the medical condition has been resolved because the dog has learned that eliminating in the house is more convenient than going outside.

Urinary incontinence—a lack of voluntary control over the passage of urine—is sometimes difficult to distinguish from submissive or excitement urination. This problem is most common in spayed or elderly female dogs. It appears to be caused by reduced activity of the sex hormone receptors in the urethral muscle.

The bottom line

Aggression, anxiety disorders, housesoiling and compulsive behaviours are all relatively common in companion and working dogs. Concluding that these are true *behaviour problems* is almost always a diagnosis by default.

The animal's veterinarian should definitely be consulted so that possible physical causes are first ruled out. Attempting to alter behaviour through modification techniques can be extremely frustrating for both the dog and the owner if there is an underlying, untreated organic cause for the objectionable behaviour.

Sometimes an unsound body can lead to an unsound mind.

2011 update 1

Further studies have looked at the role of serotonin in canine aggression. A group of researchers in Spain compared dogs with a history of aggression toward people with control dogs that had no history of aggression. They specifically measured serum concentration levels of serotonin (5-HT) and a serotonin transporter (5-HTT). The concentration of 5-HT in the blood was lower and the rate of 5-HT uptake through the transporter was higher in the aggressive dogs. This suggests that selective serotonin reuptake inhibitors, such as Fluoxetine (Prozac), that increase levels of circulating serotonin, should have an impact on aggression. A further study, conducted by the same researchers, examined the effects of a thirty-day treatment of Fluoxetine on levels of serotonin and the stress hormone, cortisol. They administered Fluoxetine to dogs with a history of aggression toward people and to laboratory Beagles with no history of aggression. In this study both groups of dogs had similar concentrations of serotonin prior to being administered the Fluoxetine. The aggressive dogs, however, had higher levels of cortisol. After treatment with Fluoxetine, the results were mixed. Levels of serotonin in the blood were lower for both aggressive and control dogs. There was no difference in cortisol between the two groups of dogs. Owners of the aggressive dogs reported improved behaviour. The upshot is that further research may determine that baseline serum levels of serotonin and cortisol may predict the likelihood of an animal responding favourably to pharmacologic treatment.

2011 update 2

To date, behaviourists and veterinary behaviourists have not provided convincing evidence that treatment for hypothyroidism resolves aggressive behaviour. While there are a handful of case studies that suggests thyroid treatment is beneficial, there are still no controlled studies documenting a direct link between hypothyroidism and aggression. One study contrasted thyroid levels for dogs with a history of aggressive behaviour and dogs lacking such a history and no difference was reported.

DANGEROUS DOGS

A Coroner's Inquest

At the time I wrote this column, I had just finished testifying at the coroner's inquest into the death of eight year old Courtney Trempe. In April 1998, Courtney, while playing in a neighbour's yard in suburban Toronto, was bitten by a Bull Mastiff named Mosley and died shortly thereafter. The purpose of the inquest was to examine the circumstances surrounding Courtney's death and to generate recommendations that would help prevent such an incident from happening again.

A fatal dog bite—the mere thought strikes dread into our hearts. How could things go so wrong that a dog would be capable of killing a child? Canada has seen at least four fatalities by dogs in the past two years, with several more close calls. The average annual death toll from dog bites in the US is eighteen. Sadly, most of the victims are children, like Courtney.

Which dogs bite?

Epidemiological studies of *severe* dog bites reveal that the majority of biters are un-neutered male purebreds. Most of the bites are committed by young dogs (older than six months but less than five years of age) of large breeds.

Dogs that bite are more likely to be family pets than strays. Most serious bites occur on the dog owner's property or directly adjacent to it. Only two percent of all reported dog bites occur in public parks.

Dogs that bite are more likely to be tied or otherwise restrained. Most portentous, these dogs usually have a history of aggressive behaviour.

Who are the victims of dog bites?

I found it shocking to learn that as many as forty-five percent of children have been bitten by a dog by their twelfth birthday. Boys between the ages of five and nine years are the most likely recipients of serious dog bites. Bites are typically directed to the face and extremities. Victims of severe dog bites are usually running or struggling at the time of the attack. In the majority of cases where children are bitten, an adult was in close proximity.

One study reported that, with the exception of "Pit Bulls," the majority of bites were provoked, meaning that the dog was interacting with the person prior to the bite. Sixty percent of bites by Pit Bulls were classified as unprovoked.

What motivates dangerous dogs?

Fortunately, most displays of aggression by dogs are not intended to cause serious injury and so, the bites are inhibited. Some forms of aggression, however, lead to a more volatile situation. For instance, aggression designed to defend a territory can be exceedingly treacherous, if the person is located within the dog's spatial boundaries. Threatening behaviours typically precede a territorial attack. Dogs that treat humans as prey are extremely dangerous as they display uninhibited biting with no warning. Predatory aggression is also enhanced by group behaviour and general arousal.

In one case reported in the literature, a pack of dogs was seen chasing a deer a few minutes prior to the dogs encountering a young boy. The dogs were already in a high state of arousal and tragically redirected their predatory behaviour onto the boy.

Frustrative aggression, which is often enhanced by restraint, can also have dire consequences if the dog is released or the victim unwittingly strays into the dog's area. A child who habitually teases a dog through a fence is a prime target if the gate is somehow unlatched.

Legal and moral responsibility

It is amazing how few dog owners in Canada are familiar with the Dog Owner's Liability Act. This Act holds the owner of a dog responsible for the dog's actions regardless of the specific details of the attack, even if the victim wanders onto the owner's property. I recently spoke with the owner of a dog that had seriously injured a child when the child entered his backyard to retrieve a toy. The owner felt he should not be accountable because the dog was contained by a fence (and an unlocked gate!).

In a case in the US, a conviction of manslaughter was delivered when the prosecution showed that the owner encouraged the dogs' aggressive behaviour and knowingly contained the dogs in an inadequate fence from which the dogs escaped and killed a child.

How can tragedies be prevented?

Are dangerous dogs born or created? Studies suggest that few, if any, behaviours are purely innate or purely learned. Instead, behaviour is believed to represent a complex interplay between genetics and life experience. By way of analogy, the genetic makeup of the animal dictates the 'rules' of a game of chess, while experience influences the precise "moves" within the game.

Breeders can make an important contribution toward eliminating dangerous dogs by selecting for stable, sociable temperaments in their lines. This will ensure that the basic framework for good behaviour is there. The rest of the job must be done by owners, and therefore, education is the key. Breeders, veterinarians, dog professionals, and fanciers of every ilk must educate the public about socialization and training, good management practices, and warning signs for aggression. Children, in particular, should be taught as part of their school curriculum how to behave with both friendly and unfriendly dogs. Young children should *never* be left alone with a dog, no matter how gentle and reliable the animal.

One suggestion made at the Trempe inquest was for a breed 'rating' system, of the same flavour as ratings on films and music. Each rating could be based on a formula which incorporates such factors as the size of the breed, the purpose for which it was developed (i.e., aggression toward people, other animals, etc.), trainability, and so forth. Unlike breed-specific legislation, this program would not restrict the ownership of any specific breed but, rather, would require that veterinarians inform new owners that they need to undertake additional efforts to socialize, train and control certain breeds more than others.

A common crusade

The frightening reality is that the only way to be sure that no child ever again dies as a result of a dog bite is to ban all dogs. We must guard against such radical directives by taking every opportunity to assist and educate the public about the dog's behavioural needs and the important contributions of dogs in our society.

That a tragedy, such as the one faced by the Trempe family, never occurs again must be our common crusade.

I'm Listening
1-800-BAD-DOGS

Dr. Pam Addresses the Most Common Behaviour Problems

"Do you always seem to be finding the wrong dog? Is your favorite pooch driving you nuts? Do you need help with your canine family? Then dial 1-800-BAD-DOGS and speak live to Dr. Pam for all your relationship questions. Now, you won't receive any spiritual or moral counseling, just practical advice on forming and maintaining good relations with all the important dogs in your life. Again that's 1-800-BAD-DOGS. Call now—the lines are open."

Q: Zack, our Portuguese Water Dog, has become increasingly difficult to walk. As soon as he hears the jingle of tags from a dog's collar, he gets very excited. When he sees the dog, he stops dead in his tracks and waits. As the dog nears, he lowers himself into a crouch and then springs into action. He lunges at the dog, barking and snarling, and it's all I can do to hold him back. One time he pulled free and attacked a Labrador Retriever—she needed three stitches in her ear. A neighbour saw me and suggested we use a pinch collar and that helps a bit. The weird thing is that he's fine at the park. He even plays with dogs. I don't understand him at all!

Dr. Pam: Some dogs develop what's called leash-induced aggression. It seems to be based in frustration. More often than not, Zack never gets to meet the dogs he encounters on the street. What may have started off as playful curiosity and sociability has become aggression because of his annoyance that he doesn't get to interact. Added to the frustration is that, whenever he does pull toward a dog, he receives a painful correction to his neck from the pinch collar. No doubt you also signal your concern about the other dog by tightening up on Zack's leash. Now you've got three factors that make Zack intensely dislike passing dogs on the street. I recommend that, for the next month or so, you drive him to the park so he doesn't have this unpleasant experience.

Get him accustomed to wearing a halter (head collar) so that when you do start walking him on-leash again, you'll have more control over him physically and he won't be receiving those painful jerks from the pinch collar. When you begin walking him again, vary your route. Carry plenty of his favourite treats. The second he sees a dog or hears the jingle of collar tags, pull out a handful of the treats and entice him to chase your fist to nibble at the treats. Don't give him pieces—instead, he should be focused on working to get them out of your fist. Pick up the pace so that he enjoys this routine. Make sure he gets enough of the treats to keep trying. As the other dog gets closer, veer off to the side so you won't have to tighten the leash. Keep moving! Continue the game until the other dog has passed you. Then put the treats away and carry on until the next dog comes along. Zack will learn that approaching dogs means treats for him and those treats come from you so his attention will be focused on you rather than the dog.

Q. Dr. Pam, please help me. I don't know what to do. I live with an 8-month-old Golden Retriever named Molly. She's just the sweetest dog except for one thing: she's aggressive over chew bones. She's done this ever since we first got her as a baby. Last week, she nipped our son when he walked by her. We're thinking of returning her to the breeder. Is that the right decision?

Dr. Pam: Some puppies naturally guard valued resources. Presumably they learned this behaviour while in the litter. It's important to address the tendency right away. Sit and hold the chewie for the puppy. Occasionally remove it from the pup's mouth and smear some peanut butter on it and give it back. Do this whether the puppy growls or not—you don't want to confirm her suspicions that you are competing for the bone. If you plan to give the puppy a chewie to keep, only give a small one that she can finish in one sitting.

Most puppies will quickly learn that when you're around you can actually take the bone and make it taste better! Seek professional help if the puppy becomes more aggressive. Without intervention, guarding behaviour is likely to get worse. With an older puppy, treatment is a bit more risky, especially if she has shown herself capable of biting. You can start off by tossing treats to her as you walk by while she's chewing a bone. Give her plenty of chewies so they become less valuable to her. *Never* take an unfinished chewie away from her—if it's safe to do so, take it away, make it better and give it back, but always let her finish it or at least, trade her for a handful of treats.

Q: Dr. Pam, thank you in advance for your help. I have a delightful little Wire-haired Fox Terrier named Max that displays a disturbing behaviour. Each time we come home from a walk or a trip to the park, he gets this imploring look in his eyes and he latches onto my leg and starts humping! If I let him, he'll do it for a few seconds and then he's fine. If I don't let him, he keeps bugging me for about five minutes and then he seems to give up. He was neutered at seven months of age and I never see him mounting other dogs. Is this a sign of dominance? Should I be worried?

Dr. Pam: You describe your dog as "delightful," which leads me to assume that you're not having any other problems with Max. If that's true, then I doubt you need to be concerned. Dogs mount and thrust for a variety of reasons—for some, it's a form of sexual behaviour; for others, it's a component of play. Some dogs mount because, before they were neutered, they learned it felt good. And yes, some dogs mount to intimidate or control others. Mounting as a form of dominance would be highly unlikely to happen in isolation of other annoying behaviours. Given that Max wants to mount after an exciting trip to the park, he is probably just aroused and mounting and thrusting helps him feel calmer. You can try redirecting him to a bone so he can relax through chewing or, if you don't mind him humping, try placing a large stuffed toy between Max and your leg. Hopefully, he'll learn to like humping the toy instead!

Q: We had a baby ten months ago and our Doberman, Pal, was uninterested in her until she started to crawl. Now Pal is quite frightened of her. He'll stay in the same room with us if she's in my arms but he paces a lot. If I put her on the floor, he leaves the room and hides under the dining-room table. I really wanted us to be a family but Pal really doesn't like her. He's always been a high-strung dog.

Dr. Pam: Well, I won't mince words—you're in a tough situation here. The good news is that Pal has adopted the behaviour of avoiding the baby in a situation where some dogs would choose to respond aggressively. The bad news is that it's going to be a challenge to convince Pal that the baby is fun to be around, especially as he is a nervous dog, because babies move erratically and make lots of noise. I would encourage Pal to stick around the baby while she's in her high chair and let him to clean up any food that gets thrown about. Instead of feeding Pal his meals in a bowl, place the baby in some type of restraint, such as a playpen, and hand feed Pal near the baby. Reinforce him for approaching her whenever she's restrained and for avoiding her when she's mobile. My worry is that Pal might bite if he ever feels he can't get away from the baby. Pull your furniture away from walls and corners so that Pal has plenty of escape routes. Establish high places where Pal can get away from the baby, rather than underneath the table—the baby could easily trap him under there. If you ever suspect Pal could snap at or bite the baby, seek the assistance of a certified animal behaviourist or veterinary behaviourist.

Q: Hello, Dr. Pam. I'm very frustrated. I live alone with Ciara, a three-year-old active and playful Bouvier des Flandres. She's especially exuberant when people come to my door. This 80-pound dog jumps up on guests and tries to lick them in the face. My trainer suggested that I have plenty of people come over and repeatedly come in and out while I teach her to sit and stay. This is not feasible for me—I don't have much company and those that I do have are not interested in helping me train her. What else can I do?

Dr. Pam: How wonderful to have such a social butterfly for a companion! Your trainer gave you excellent advice—this procedure is very effective because the repeated visits eventually cause the dog to calm down, making it more likely that she will be able to comply with your wishes. I do understand your dilemma, though. An alternative that might work, because Ciara is so playful, is to redirect her from the guests to a special toy. Some dogs are so excited and aroused when people come to visit that they just have to jump and kiss. Each time you come in, right away offer Ciara a toy that she doesn't normally get to play with. Play a game of tug and then encourage her to run around the house with the toy.

Once she has the idea of taking out her enthusiasm on the toy, leave the toy near the door. When you come home, cue her to grab the toy as she comes running to greet you. The next step is to transfer this behaviour to when guests come in the door. Many dogs will actually begin to search for the toy, unprompted, so they can show it off. An added benefit is that many dogs won't jump up if they have an object in their mouth. I am always reluctant to use any type of unpleasant method to discourage jumping up on people, such as kneeing the dog or stepping on the dog's toes, because you don't want to dampen the dog's desire to socialize with people. Far too many dogs have the problem of not being friendly enough to guests!

At most, I might suggest that you have Ciara wear a training collar and a leash when guests arrive. If she chooses to jump up rather than play with the toy, the guest can step on the leash so Ciara will administer her own correction by hitting the end of the leash. Remind

Ciara to either sit or grab her toy. This procedure still requires some cooperation from your guests but Ciara may get the message more quickly.

Q: Dr. Pam, thank you for taking my call. We own a seven-month-old Chinese Shar-Pei that is destroying our home! We can't leave Q alone because he digs at the doors and the surrounding trim and pulls up the carpet. We're at our wit's end! We tried putting him in a crate but he digs at the crate until his paws bleed and, one day, he broke a tooth chewing at the wire door. When we're home, Q's great. Please help!

Dr. Pam: It sounds as though Q is suffering from a classic case of separation anxiety, meaning that he becomes distraught when isolated from his family. I can only give you a few tips in this short time so I encourage you to seek the assistance of a certified animal behaviourist or veterinary behaviourist for more thorough guidance. You will want to protect your home from further damage while you work with Q. Cover the door with Plexiglas, spray the chewed woodwork with Bitter Apple, and place a Scat Mat on the floor to discourage Q from going close to the door.

Practice leaving for very short periods of time—maybe just a few seconds to start. If Q is too anxious, you may need to get him used to the new routine outside a bathroom or bedroom door first. Leave him with a Kong stuffed with wonderful treats like cheese or peanut butter. When you return, even if you've only been gone for a few seconds, remove the Kong so Q learns that he gets the special treat only when you're not there. Gradually build up the time you wait on the other side of the door, making sure to incorporate some really short times so that you're not always making it harder for him. If Q refuses to eat if you make any motions toward the door at all, you may want to speak with your veterinarian about a short-term course of an anti-anxiety medication. Separation anxiety is tough to work through but most dogs do get over it with treatment.

Q: Hi Dr. Pam. What can you do about a puppy that pees all over the floor every time you go to pet her? We have a five-month-old Cocker Spaniel and I have to totally ignore her or I end up with pee all over my shoes! I've tried spanking her but if anything, it's getting worse. She's pretty well housetrained at other times.

Dr. Pam: I suspect you're dealing with a case of submissive urination. You sound like a big guy with a deep voice and you may come across as frightening to a small puppy. Puppies tend to flip upside-down and urinate when they feel threatened—among dogs, this is a way of saying, "Don't hurt me, I mean no harm." The glitch is that you mustn't punish her because the urination will get worse if you do. She'll try even harder to appease you. What you can do is: 1) interact with her outside where you don't care if she pees; 2) try not to lean over her—instead, sit on the floor, make yourself small, and use a high, squeaky voice; and 3) distract her by tossing treats on the floor so she's more likely to search for the treats than grovel to you. The good news is that most puppies grow out of this behaviour by the time they're about one year old.

Q: Dr. Pam, boy, do I have a problem! Our Sheltie is driving us nuts with his barking. He barks at people, animals, noises—he just barks non-stop! He can't stay in the backyard because the neighbours complain about the noise. When he's inside, he lays at the top of the stairs where he can see out the front window. The instant he sees anyone, he sounds the alarm and races back and forth from window to window. And we rarely have company anymore because he barks so much we can't even hold a conversation. Yelling at him doesn't work, spanking him doesn't work, even spraying him with water doesn't work—he thinks that's a game. Is there anything we can do?

Dr. Pam: A barking Sheltie? What a surprise! Some breeds are more prone to barking than others and, unfortunately, you have chosen a breed that ranks high on the barking scale! So it's important to set realistic goals. You can't curb the barking completely. Instead, your focus should be on teaching your Sheltie to stop when you tell him, "That's enough." There are a few things that I think will help. First, it sounds as though your Sheltie needs a job. These dogs are highly intelligent workaholics and your dog has generated his own job description. Make sure he gets plenty of exercise, off his own property, where he is exposed to all the sights and sounds of the community. When he's home, keep him busy with toys you can stuff with food, and play games. Block off the windows so he can't play 'guard dog.' Play the stereo or TV so you mask much of the outside sounds.

Try reinforcing incompatible behaviour when he does start to bark. Respond consistently after one or two barks: say, "That's enough" and call him to you, place him in a sit- or down-stay, and, after thirty to sixty seconds of quiet, reward him. Gradually increase the quiet time required to get a treat. You run the risk of teaching him to bark even more frequently to get your attention and the treats but at the same time, you'll be teaching him to stop barking on request. Make sure you also reward him anytime he inhibits barking at something that would normally set him off. Ideally, he'll figure out to come to you every time he hears something, in anticipation of the treats.

If this training procedure is too labour-intensive or is ineffective, you may need to consider an anti-bark collar. There are several that have been shown to be effective. One of the available types works on a microphone system, which can be a problem if you have more than one dog because the dog not wearing the collar can trigger the device! When the dog barks, the sound activates the collar to spray a harmless but unpleasant mist of citronella in the dog's face.

The advantage of using an anti-bark collar is that everything is done automatically, so you don't have to worry about issues like timing, consistency and so forth. However, most dogs become 'collar-wise,' in that they inhibit barking only while wearing the collar. This is actually a blessing in disguise because I would recommend that you set aside times during the day when it's okay for your Sheltie to bark. Take the collar off and let him go wild! This way he gets the opportunity to bark, which is highly reinforcing to him.

"Well, that's all the time we have for today. We hope you've enjoyed the show and, if you couldn't get through, please try again tomorrow."

Saying Good-bye to Old Friends

There Are Ways to Ease the Loss

There are few experiences sadder than watching a loved one succumb to the ravages of age. Life with an aging dog is an emotional wave of ups and downs, marked by the memories of a vibrant, healthy animal and the reality of providing palliative care.

This column is extremely difficult for me to write as I recently bid my eleven year old Border Collie, Ciaran, a fond farewell, and I am now facing the imminent death of my beloved fourteen year old Saluki, Shaahiin. Ciaran's illness manifested itself in the course of only a few days so I was unprepared for his loss. The experience certainly brought home to me just how precious the time is that I have left with Shaahiin.

Making the decision

It is rarely easy to make the decision to euthanize an old dog, even though the goal is to prevent or end suffering. Given that 70 per cent of American pet owners report that they think of their pets as children, it's not surprising that people with elderly animals are distraught with grief, confusion, and guilt at the prospect of making that final appointment with the veterinarian.

How do people determine when it is the right time? I have asked this question of many dog lovers in the past few months, prompted by my concern over Shaahiin's mental and physical well-being. Some wait until the dog appears to be withdrawing, others wait until the dog is no longer able to move around, others wait until the dog starts soiling itself, and still others look for the sparkle to leave the dog's eyes. Several expressed regret at waiting too long; no one felt they had euthanized too early.

Rites of passage

Some people find it comforting to offer the dog special experiences in the final few days. The dog might enjoy a last supper of carefully prepared steak or a relaxing night's sleep snuggled in the owner's bed. Ciaran's favorite thing in the world was to herd sheep but, as an urban dog, he hadn't been near a sheep in years. On his last evening, we visited a farm and, even though he couldn't move, I like to think that for a few moments he forgot his pain as he stood transfixed outside the sheep pen.

Others find solace in death rituals. I like to imagine that some day I might scatter Ciaran's ashes over the lake district of England. Our first Saluki lies in a grave in Nebraska on the plains where she used to hunt. When I think of her, I always envision her there, standing with ears alert, eyes searching for the slightest movement of a hare. Some people post a public farewell by publishing an obituary, perhaps in a breed or sport magazine or on the internet. Others plant a special flower, bush or tree. Still others prefer the permanence of burial in a pet cemetery.

The role of the veterinarian

The veterinarian can have an enormous impact on the euthanasia experience for the family. I have heard horror stories of people bringing their suffering pet in for the euthanasia appointment, only to sit for several hours in the waiting room or be sent home because of an over-booked schedule. More and more people are opting for euthanasia at home, where the dog is comfortable and relaxed and the family can grieve away from the public eye.

Families may choose to conduct a formal funeral for their dog. I read about a special veterinarian who offers her clients a customized ceremony. She sends a blanket home with the client and asks that the dog be on the blanket, in its favourite spot in the house, when she arrives. She gives the dog a sedative to relax it and, while the drug takes effect, she lights a white candle and says a prayer. Family members say their farewells and the veterinarian gives the final medication. The dog is wrapped in the blanket while a passage is read from the book *Good-bye, My Friend: Grieving the Loss of a Pet* (Montgomery and Montgomery, 1991). The veterinarian writes a dedication to the dog inside the cover of the book, and leaves the book with the family to help them during the bereavement period.

Euthanasia in the clinic can also be a peaceful, reverent experience. It's best to schedule the appointment for the end of the day, when the reception area is relatively empty and the veterinarian can take his time. If at all possible, make arrangements for disposal of the body *prior* to the appointment. The family should be brought into the room immediately, rather than being asked to wait in reception. A soft bed and blanket for the dog, combined with dim lighting, will make the surroundings less clinical. Ideally, the veterinarian will do his best to recede into the background, while at the same time conveying compassion for the family's loss. The family should always be given as much private time with the body as they need. Send a sympathy card and bill at a later date.

Research indicates that even if the owners choose not to be present for the euthanasia, it's helpful that they view the body for the reality to sink in. This is especially important if there are children in the family.

Do other animals in the home need to see the body? No one has a clear answer for this question. I've heard stories of dogs that acted as though they were searching for their friend, but this behaviour ceased after they were permitted to sniff the body. Some dogs do exhibit behavioural changes, including severe depression and even anorexia after the death of a companion, while other dogs show no apparent recognition of the loss. Ciaran and my young dog were virtually inseparable, yet the only change in Eejit's behaviour seems to be that he directs more play toward me in situations where he previously would have tried to engage Ciaran.

Paying tribute

There is no denying that some people do not recognize the gravity of bereavement that pet owners go through when they lose a beloved dog. Despite the fact that there are veterinarians and psychologists who make pet loss their focus of study, some mental-health professionals even fail to grasp that pets can be mourned with the same intensity that family and friends are mourned. I am incensed when I hear that a grieving pet owner is advised to "Get over it, it was only a dog" or "Can't you get another?" Grieving pet owners go through the same stages of grief as anyone else—anger, guilt, depression, and, finally, acceptance. Some find it helpful to introduce a new dog into the family fairly quickly; for others, this would not be appropriate.

Because of the lack of understanding that many grieving pet owners face, I feel it is especially important for those of us who do understand to acknowledge the mourning of our friends. Send a card or make a telephone call. It helps to hear from people who have been there themselves. I learned of a particularly touching tribute when a friend lost her dear Golden Retriever, Chester, a few months ago. Her co-worker contacted a star-charting company and presented her with a lovely framed certificate proclaiming the existence of a star in the night sky named Chester.

Shaahiin and Ciaran.

The gift of release

Celebrating our cherished seniors is, sadly, tainted by the knowledge of their limited time with us. The final gift we can bestow upon these animals, as they reach the end of their lives, is a painless release, a dignity we are forbidden to offer our fellow human beings. I pray that I will know the right time for my precious Shaahiin.

ABOUT THE AUTHOR

Pamela Reid's a trained scientist with a PhD in animal learning and behavior. She understands research and she can tell good work from bad. Better yet, she can *translate* scientific theories and findings into comprehensible language, sharing where and how the research is relevant to the real world.

Pam's a certified behaviorist. She's consulted on thousands of cases over the years, working with everything from an attack cat whose owner had to call 911 to a suicidal dog who leapt out a third story window, convincing his owners that the house was haunted. She evaluates dogs that have seriously injured or killed people. She even participated in a murder investigation for which the defense argued that the dog did the killing.

Pam's a dog trainer. She started with an unlikely breed, a remarkable Saluki named Shaahiin. Shaahiin earned his Novice and Open titles, winning breed and group awards for high scores. They went on to Flyball, where Shaahiin became the first and he remained the *only* Saluki to earn a Flyball Dog Championship for the following 15 years. They tackled agility where Shaahiin was the first Saluki to earn a USDAA Agility Dog title. Pam's next dog was Ciaran the Border Collie, who racked up titles in obedience, flyball, and agility. Ciaran won numerous Grand Prix events and classes at the USDAA Nationals. Pam's best buddy is still her Border-Border Eejit, a veritable legend in agility. Eejit, now 16 years old, is a two-time USDAA National Steeplechase Champion, and a three-time USDAA Regional DAM Team Champion. Pam is now focused on teaching her young lurcher, Snafu, to love the game as much as Eejit does. Clearly Pam knows dog training. She knows how to teach, she knows how to motivate, she knows how to refine, and she knows how to compete to get the best out of the team.

Recommended Reading

The Culture Clash, 2nd Ed. by Jean Donaldson. James and Kenneth, 2005.

Dogs: A New Understanding of Canine Origin, Behavior, and Evolution by Raymond and Lorna Coppinger. University of Chicago Press, 2001.

Dominance in Dogs. Fact or Fiction by Barry Eaton. Dogwise Publishing, 2011

Don't Shoot the Dog 2nd ed. by Karen Pryor. Bantam Books, 1999.

Excel-Erated Learning by Pamela Reid. James and Kenneth, 1996.

Genetics and the Social Behavior of the Dog by John Paul Scott and John L. Fuller. University of Chicago Press, 1965.

Mine! by Jean Donaldson. Dogwise Publishing, 2002.

The New Knowledge of Dog Behavior by Clarence Pfaffenberger. Dogwise Publishing, 1963.

The Intelligence of Dogs by Stanley Coren. Free Press, 2005.

Oh Behave! by Jean Donaldson. Dogwise Publishing, 2008.

On Talking Terms with Dogs, 2nd Ed. by Turid Rugaas. Dogwise Publishing, 2006.

Ruff Love by Susan Garrett. Clean Run Productions, 2002.

"Some Genetic and Endocrine Effects of Selection for Domestication in Silver Foxes" by D.K. Belyaev and L.N Trut. In *The Wild Canids,* edited by Michael W. Fox. Dogwise Publishing, 2009 reprint.

Successful Dog Adoptions by Sue Sternberg. Howell Book House, 2003.